JONNY TRUNK

Hi-Fi brochures 1950s–1980s

FUEL

Back in 1981 I got run over by a motorbike. It was a 400cc Honda with rider and pillion passenger. Miraculously no one was hurt, but it was a shocking moment for the general public, going about their business outside the hi-fi shop on the Grosvenor Road, Aldershot.

Having been taught road safety by The Green Cross Code Man, this was a most unusual incident for me. However, things had changed completely that week. I'd bought a Sony Walkman a few days earlier and found myself totally lost in the sound of 'Jungle Strut' by The Square (a track from the Sony Demonstration Cassette that came free with the Walkman). Wired for sound and deaf to the noise of the traffic, I had simply 'strutted' right into the road without looking – or even caring. Bang! Clatter!

The Sony Walkman was a magic invention. The perfect poppy, portable, personal sound machine. According to legend, it was invented by the founder of Sony, Masaru Ibuka, when he spotted a guy at a Tokyo station, walking along holding a large ghetto blaster with a pair of headphones attached. He thought to himself: 'that would be better if the cassette player was smaller'. This may be an apocryphal story, but I like it anyway. The Walkman II I'd bought with hard-earned, saved-up cash, came with a belt hook – as well as cool-looking, comfortable headphones (these even had a button to mute the sound if you ever needed to hear the outside world). Supremely modern in its styling, it included a spare battery pack, so I could listen for hours on end. The Walkman II was the first piece of audio tech I'd bought myself and seemed like a big step up from the 'Elizabethan' (that's the brand, not the period) portable record player, a clunky orange machine that we played *The Sound of Music* LP on at home. It was a truly modern twist on the old portable transistor and classic cassette recorder that I used to tape rubbish off the telly.

Tru-Fi – the shop that sold me the Walkman – was a lively modern hi-fi emporium, with slightly dimmed lighting so when you walked in all the hi-fi fascia lights would glow seductively. The staff weren't as snooty as they were at Lloyd and Keyworth, the posh hi-fi shop in Farnham ('don't touch that young man!'), and they were happy for me and my chums to come in and look excitedly around. One friend had an airline pilot dad and because he was away all the time, he'd load up his son with guilt cash, the bulk of which was spent in KFC, the local arcade and Tru-Fi.

Post-Walkman, my cassette fixation developed into an obsession with vinyl, which in turn transferred to mix tapes. I moved into low end (and just about affordable) hi-fi separates: an entry level, solid green plastic NAD turntable with a smoked plastic lid, a fat Sony amplifier with a big volume knob, a Technics double tape deck and some cheap, wood-encased no name speakers. When I look back at the compilation tapes I made for the car / for love / for birthdays, I found this technology to be totally functional, it worked just perfectly for my needs (although I'm not sure I ever fully understood what was going on with the little metal / chrome switch on the cassette recorder).

By the early 1990s, when it had become clear I was a record collector, everything had been updated. Much of the music I was listening to was from the 1960s and 1970s, so I tried to keep my home set up based around equipment from that period. I bought a Quad 33 / 303 set in 1991 from a vintage retailer in Tottenham Court Road (when the whole road was hi-fi heaven), followed by a Thorens TD124 MK2 at a Dartmouth auction in 1990 for £12, and a few weeks later, a pair of Celestion speakers from a scary, fetishist, husband and wife hi-fi shop in Shepherd's Bush. It all still works perfectly for me and sounds amazing – the only parts I've changed in the last

elizabethan

What a wonderful range

BRAUN   Lautsprechereinheiten

thirty-odd years are some cables (a questionable improvement) and a small belt for the turntable and the stylus. Although I was also forced (by myself) to buy a Sound Burger, on page 9 – because they are totally cool and were (and still are) THE portable to take to record fairs. It was expensive, but you recoup your money pretty fast by not buying terrible singles, as you can hear them before you take them home.

The fact that my home set up has remained virtually unchanged in nearly four decades has not prevented me from looking at alternatives. I've seen the extremes of hi-fidelity over the years, from giant-size 1920s Western Electric horns to weird-looking and obscenely priced contemporary audiophile gear, complete with cables that cost more than my entire system. I love checking out classic turntables, weird cassette decks and quirky, failed hi-fi ideas. Every so often I visit the Audio Jumble in Tonbridge and most weeks I'll scroll through sold hi-fi items on eBay. Which is where the germ of an idea for this book started.

The brochures in this book are presented alphabetically by brand name, but what I didn't realise when I began collecting them was that – inadvertently – they would also reveal the history of home listening. Post-war it was an engineering task to build a viable music system at home. This was a highly specialised undertaking, involving a proficient grasp of engineering and electronics. You'd maybe buy your valve amp from Quad, then a 'platter' turntable (plinth not included) from Thorens, a stylus from Dual and speaker cones from Rogers Development. Then you'd have to build housing cabinets and wire it all together. Most equipment came with paper templates and technical drawings to help with the cabinet work and stylus placing (there were even cabinet companies ready to help out if required, see Hill-Craft on page 95). Reel to reel tape was also a very popular mode of listening in the early years, which explains the sheer number of these machines in the book.

Early tape machines and DIY platters slowly gave way to the more affordable and straightforward Dansette, reel to reels, portable tape players (for 8-track) and the inexorable rise of the commercial giant that was the music centre. We have the arrival of the cassette, followed by the stack system, the micro stack system, the Walkman and finally the compact disc. Along the way I came across brochures from electric retailers that featured video, inventive TV formats and some other just plain weird stuff (chess alarm clock radio anyone?). A smattering of these are included here, as they reflect the thinking of the time.

The relentless advance of the CD seemed to coincide with the slow death of the high street hi-fi retailer. Perhaps it was because CDs were advertised as the ultimate format for conveying sound, therefore signalling the end of the search for flawless fidelity – and therefore the end of hi-fi progress. This is speculation, but I do know that all the classic hi-fi dealers and shops I used to frequent no longer exist. Luckily, a few specialists still survive and actually appear to be thriving, with renewed demand for classic (and as yet unsurpassed) systems for playing old formats. Many enthusiasts will tell you that the technology for playing vinyl, tape, cassettes and CDs reached its sonic peak decades ago. Evidence of this can be seen in the unrelenting demand for Garrard, Thorens and 1210 decks, Nakamichi tape players and classic Celestion or JBL speakers.

For obvious aesthetic reasons, Braun was one brand that was essential to include in the book. I'd found a few Braun brochures, but was aware of a whole lot more that I just couldn't track down: their print runs were small and Braun collectors guard them fiercely. Eventually, my quest led to the office of Peter Kapos at Das Programm, the extraordinary Braun archive in East London, where I spent the morning in a tech nirvana. Not only did he let me borrow some of his amazing brochure collection (pages 42–49), but he also told me a little about the history of music centres, specifically the hi-fi stack. The original blueprint for what came to be known as the 'stack system' can be traced back to HfG Ulm (aka: The Ulm School of Design). It was an idea developed by student Herbert Lindinger and his supervisor Hans Gugelot, who were both working (through the Ulm School) for the Braun Company. At the time, no one was investigating how separate audio elements could or should relate to each other spatially. Braun subsequently used Lindinger's 1958 diploma study as the basis for the modular system they produced from 1960 onwards. I think we're all better off for this knowledge.

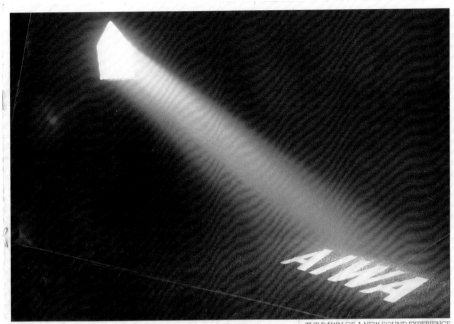

THE DAWN OF A NEW SOUND EXPERIENCE

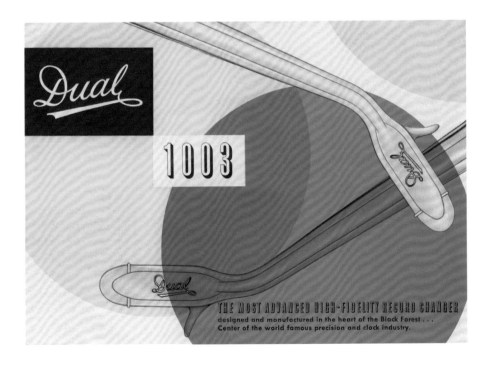

THE MOST ADVANCED HIGH-FIDELITY RECORD CHANGER
designed and manufactured in the heart of the Black Forest . . .
Center of the world famous precision and clock industry.

It was also important for me to include J.A. Michell turntables (page 120), simply because an early version of their Hydraulic Reference Turntable was used by Alex in Stanley Kubrick's *A Clockwork Orange* (1971). Apparently the version used in the film was made before the company was officially licensed. Possibly the most iconic stereo in film history, Apple guru Steve Jobs also had one. They were built by a British company that is still up and running and who were very generous and trusting, lending me their super rare 1970s brochures for the project.

This book does not claim to be a completist's guide to audio manufacturers, so you may well find some companies are missing. Many brochures were simply too dull to warrant inclusion (like Klipsch for example). Moreover, I found an inverse correlation between money and quality – often, the more expensive the equipment, the more mundane and badly produced the brochure. There are exceptions: one of these that did make it in was Peter Scheiber Sonics (page 173) where the folder opens to reveal a series of badly photocopied A4 pages with murky photos of bespoke-made, God knows what. And it's

all very expensive. There are also companies that you may never have heard of, such as Great White Whale, who sold high-end, handmade amplifiers using 18th-century whaling etchings (see below). Of course. A perfect marketing strategy.

You will also see a lot of women in this book, which was never the intention (the 'Erotica' element of the title was intended as solely as a reference to the sexy tech on show). This clearly demonstrates that throughout the last century, women were an integral part of a very lazy, male-dominated, sales process. Some examples we have included are beyond parody. My favourite has to be page 41, which could easily be a bland suburban image from the *Dressing for Pleasure* fetish book we made in 2010.

Finally, I must say special thanks to Audio Gold in North London who allowed me to pilfer their slightly crumpled stash of brochures and who also helped with the research, thanks to their unrivalled, deep knowledge of weird stereo facts and gossip.

I'm now off to put a record on. Thanks for listening.

625 and 615 Power Amplifiers

SOUND BURGER

AT727
Stereo disc player system—Instructions
Stereo-Plattenspieler—Bedienungsanleitung
Platine de tourne-disque stéréo—Mode d'emploi

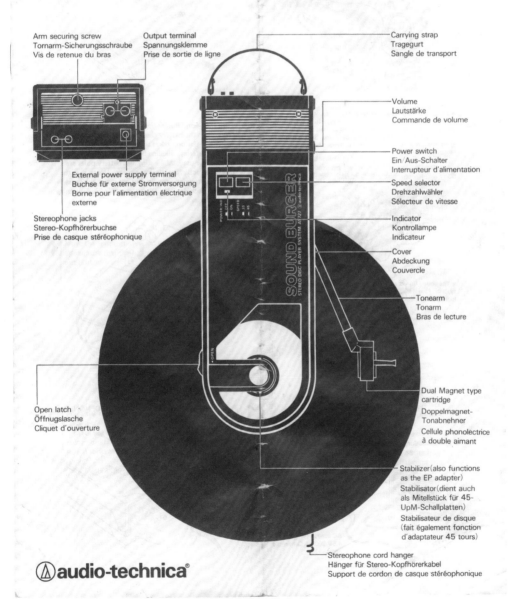

Arm securing screw
Tornarm-Sicherungsschraube
Vis de retenue du bras

Output terminal
Spannungsklemme
Prise de sortie de ligne

Carrying strap
Tragegurt
Sangle de transport

External power supply terminal
Buchse für externe Stromversorgung
Borne pour l'alimentation électrique externe

Stereophone jacks
Stereo-Kopfhörerbuchse
Prise de casque stéréophonique

Volume
Lautstärke
Commande de volume

Power switch
Ein/Aus-Schalter
Interrupteur d'alimentation

Speed selector
Drehzahlwähler
Sélecteur de vitesse

Indicator
Kontrollampe
Indicateur

Cover
Abdeckung
Couvercle

Tonearm
Tonarm
Bras de lecture

Dual Magnet type cartridge
Doppelmagnet-Tonabnehmer
Cellule phonolectrice à double aimant

Open latch
Öffnugslasche
Cliquet d'ouverture

Stabilizer(also functions as the EP adapter)
Stabilisator(dient auch als Mitellstück für 45-UpM-Schallplatten)
Stabilisateur de disque (fait également fonction d'adaptateur 45 tours)

Stereophone cord hanger
Hänger für Stereo-Kopfhörerkabel
Support de cordon de casque stéréophonique

ⓐ audio-technica®

3A

I'd always wondered what 3A referred to: well it's Art &
Acoustique Appliquée. Cool name. This French company,
established in the mid-1970s, printed the technical
data results of each speaker on the inside of the unit. The
odd, desk-like creation shown here (on the right) is their
'Triphonic' system, where the active subwoofer is hidden
in a coffee table with satellite speakers placed around the
room. Rad.

ACOUSTIC RESEARCH

AR was founded in 1954 in Cambridge, Massachusetts, by
pioneering audio geek Edgar Villchur and his student Henry
Kloss. They introduced the groundbreaking Acoustic
Suspension speaker, creating cleaner and less distorted
sound, by using an 'air spring' to hold the driver, rather
than stiff suspension. The design remains popular today.

TRIPHONIC® system

an exclusive creation of 3a

THE TRIPHONIC 800

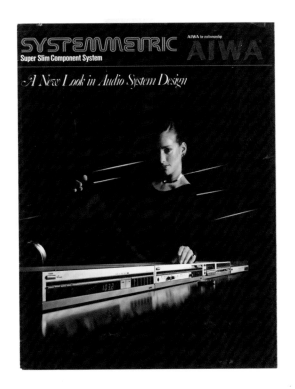

AIWA

This exciting Japanese company started out manufacturing microphones in 1951. Over the next four decades they moved into all sorts of progressive audio products (and even electric toothbrushes). After being merged into the Sony Group Corporation in 2002, the business now forms part of the Twada Corporation. Incidentally, the Walkman used by Marty McFly in *Back To The Future* is an AIWA HS-P02 Mark II.

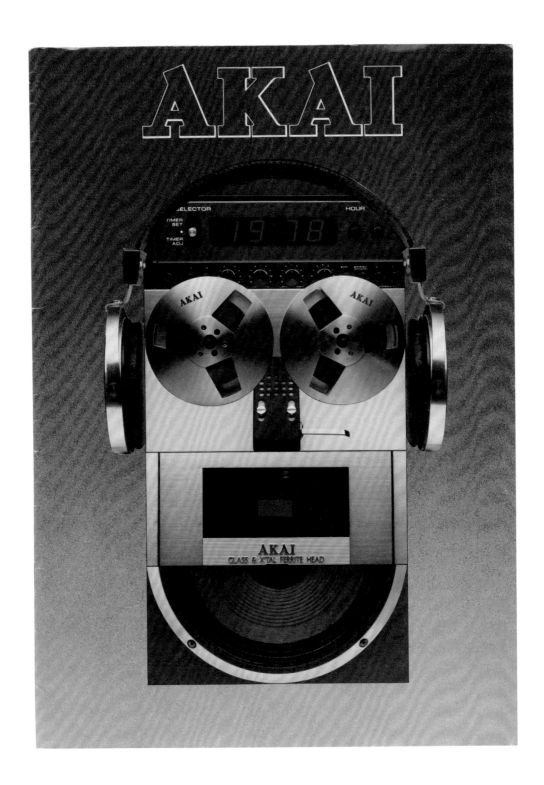

AKAI

Akai (meaning 'red' in Japanese) was founded in Japan by father and son Masukichi and Saburo Akai in 1946. This hugely innovative company produced high-quality reel to reel tape recorders, popular professional audio gear and well-designed commercial electronics for the home. Ultimately, the company filed for insolvency in 2000, after claims of dodgy accounting and theft by the chairman, assisted by one of 'The Big Four'.

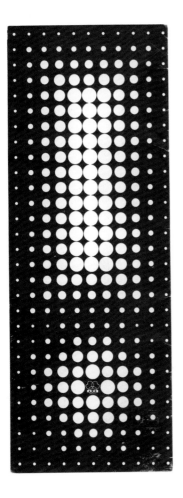

Form
und
Technik
Mikrofone

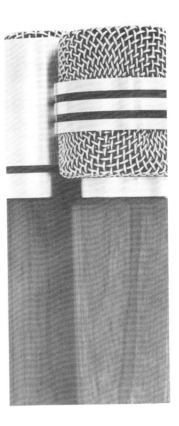

holz & metall

AKG

The Viennese company Akustische und Kino-Geräte Gesellschaft (Acoustics and Cinema Equipment) was founded in 1947, producing technical equipment for cinemas. Perhaps best-known for developing the dynamic cardioid D12 microphone in 1953, the business slowly expanded into headphones, microphones, car horns and door intercoms. In 1984 the firm was listed on the Vienna stock exchange. It is still a heavyweight industry player.

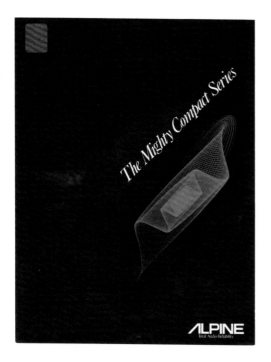

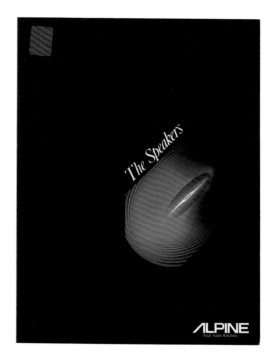

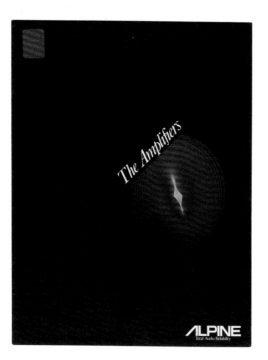

ALPINE

Originally formed as Alps-Motorola in 1967, a joint venture between Alps Electric (Japan) and Motorola (USA), the company became Alpine Electonics after a buyout in 1978. Specialising in sexy, innovative car audio systems, they developed the first in-car equaliser (1982) and in-dash CD multichanger (1993).

ALTEC
LANSING
MUSICAL
SOUND
EQUIPMENT

ALTEC LANSING

Born out of the legendary Western Electric engineering and manufacturing company in 1927, the roots of this American speaker company can be traced back to the groundbreaking audio systems that introduced the 'talkies' to cinema (with the release of *The Jazz Singer*). It had originally been named Lansing Manufacturing, after the audio-speaker whizz and founder James Bullough Lansing. When the company ran into financial trouble it was bought by Altec Manufacturing (short for 'All Technical') and Altec Lansing was born. After his contract expired in 1946, James Bullough Lansing left to form JBL. Altec Lansing still produce superb audio reproduction systems today.

Altec quality speaker systems and new stereo components are built a little better.

ALTEC
STEREO
COMPONENTS

AMPEX

The company name is derived from 'Alexander M. Poniatoff Excellence'. Poniatoff famously created the commercial reel to reel tape player for Bing Crosby, who was dissatisfied with the quality of the transcription discs (vinyl recordings made exclusively for recording radio broadcasts) used to pre-record his weekly radio show. The first commercial machine was originally developed from German wartime technology. Struggling financially to bring their prototype to market, the company was assisted with a cheque for $50,000 from Mr Crosby. The advent of the Ampex 200 was a revolutionary moment in the history of sound, recording and broadcasting. Thanks Bing.

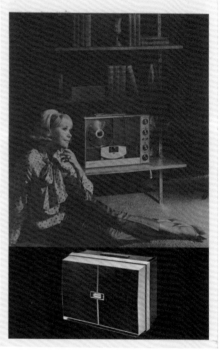

AMSTRAD

RP-10D STEREO RECORD PLAYER WITH DISCO UNIT

This stereo record player has its own built in "DISCO LIGHTS". These lights flash with the sound impulses from your record and together with a mirrored system, create an amazing lighting effect. The Disco Light unit is built into the lid and folds away completely when the record player is not being used. Variable bass, treble and balance controls are incorporated, together with sockets for stereo headphones and record/playback from an auxiliary source e.g. tape recorder. The unit comes complete with a pair of loudspeakers. They come finished in teak effect to match the trim of the record player and incorporates a 5" driver and port hole. The disco effect can be switched-off if not required leaving the unit to operate as a normal record player.

7

AUDIO RANGE 1981/82
AMSTRAD
GREAT PLAYERS

TRUTH IN LISTENING

Leistungsverstärker

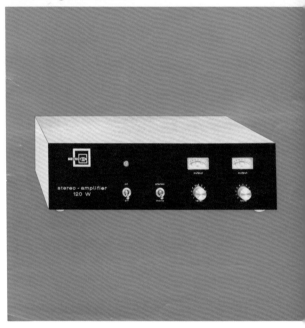

AMSTRAD

This electronics company was established by the British business magnate Alan (Michael) Sugar (**AMS Trad**ing) in 1968, when he was 21. Using injection moulding techniques Amstrad produced commercial and very affordable tech for all – my mate had the Studio 100 Cassette Multi-Mixer Turntable Radio System, which was ace. In the 1980s Amstrad moved away from audio and into the fast-growing home PC market and satellite broadcasting technologies. The firm went public in 1980 and is now owned by Sky.

AUROTON

Apart from this minimal, functional amplifier manufactured in the 1970s, I can't find anything else produced by this German company.

BELL & HOWELL

There was me thinking this legendary American movie-camera making firm just made professional and amateur film equipment. But here they are in the 1960s making daringly modern cassette devices, before forgetting all about them a few years later.

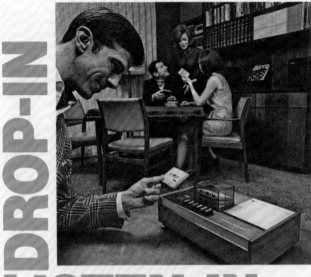

DROP-IN
LISTEN-IN
STEREO

**AUTOLOAD®
CASSETTE TAPE
STEREO DECKS AND
SYSTEMS**

BANG & OLUFSEN

The famous Danish company, known for its quality and design, was established in 1925 by Peter Bang (winner of 'the best name in this book so far') and his friend Svend Olufsen to develop technology and explore business opportunites in the audio sector. Among their early successes were loudspeakers for circuses, recording equipment for the film industry and the classic Beolit 39 radio, complete with Bakelite cabinet. During World War II, they refused to manufacture goods for Germany; as a consequence their factory was burnt down by pro-Nazi saboteurs. After rebuilding, they manufactured electric razors until 1955, when audio products were back on the menu. Employing modern progressive designers such as Ib Fabiansen and Jacob Jensen, they created an unrivalled range of sublime, desirable music systems. Based on psychoacoustic research (the human perception of audio quality) these products still look and sound superb today.

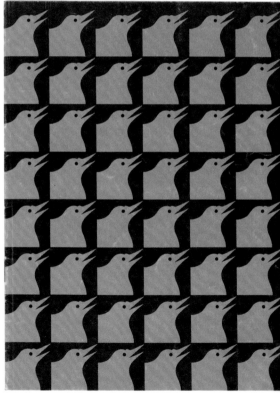

Bang&Olufsen 75/76

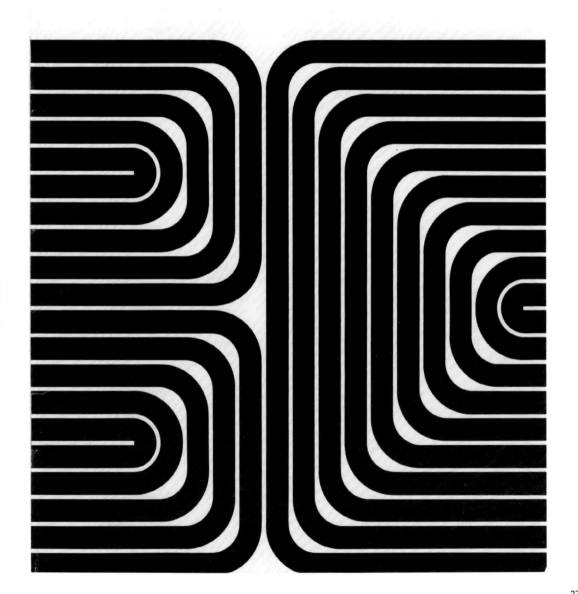

12

BEOLIT DE LUXE 611.

BEOLIT DE LUXE 611 T.

9

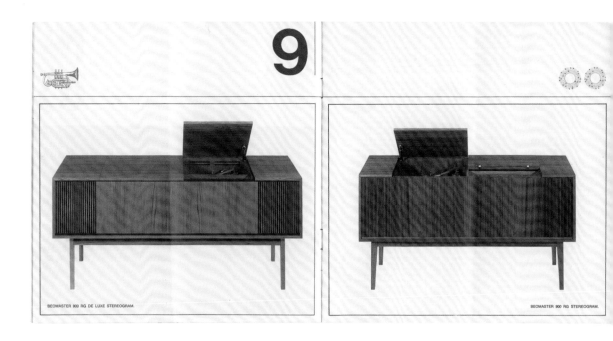

BEOMASTER 900 RG DE LUXE STEREOGRAM.

BEOMASTER 900 RG STEREOGRAM.

Bang&Olufsen High Fidelity

STEREO

System Cabinet SC 17

System Cabinet SC 50

Music Cabinet MC 40

Music Cabinet MC 30

Bang & Olufsen
Beomaster 1000/1200/1600

Beolab 8000/SC 80

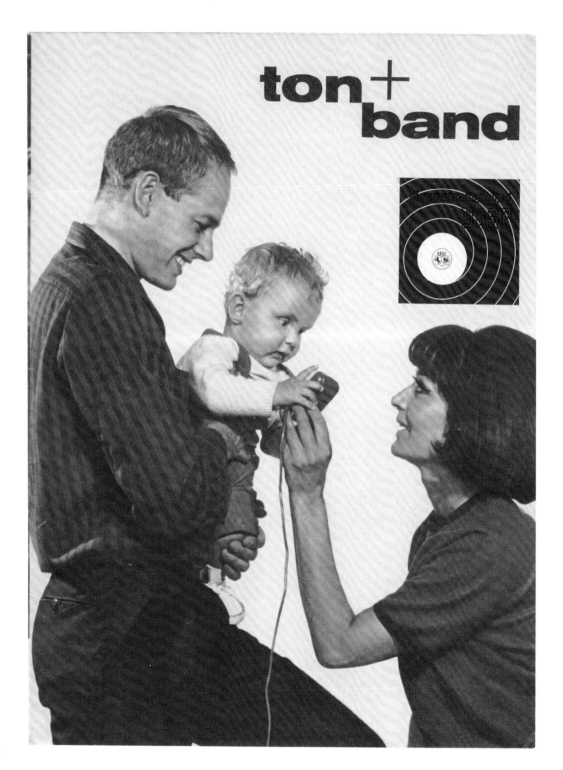

ton+
band

the tape that gives **Authentic Sound**

neu LH hifi
—das BASF Tonband LH HiFi

Häusliche
Starparade
in höchster
Tonqualität...

DOPPELSPIELBAND

730 m | 2400 feet

DOUBLE PLAYING TAPE

BASF

The initials stand for Baden Aniline and Soda Factory. Their logo has always been somewhere close in my life – oddly, there is a BASF public clock on Stoke Newington Church Street in North London. This large multinational firm has fingers in many pies and chemicals. Alongside the multitude of audio products and millions of miles of audio tape they manufactured after World War II, the company also invented the mass manufacturing of polystyrene.

MAVA 2102—8342 span. 8/71. Printed in Germany

Cinta+Sonido

BASF

Consejos para
los aficionados
a las
Compact Cassettes

BECKER

AUDIO SYSTEMS

BECKER AUDIO SYSTEMS

You know that magic button on your car stereo that automatically searches for the next radio station? Well that was
first invented back in 1953 by Becker, a fine German car
audio manufacturer, who since the 1950s have become a
global force in audio and navigation systems. The son of
founder Max Becker is called Boris, but he has never won
Wimbledon or gone to prison.

BLACK MAGIC

You may well not remember this company, but Black Magic
made a whole range of different – often quite useless –
audio and hi-fi accessories. Their LP record-cleaning
brushes always contained a conspicuous nod to the Black
Magic name. Hence the 'Magic Wand', 'Dust Wand', and
'Magic Touch' vinyl brushes. You get the idea.

BOSE

Established by Amar Bose in Massachusetts in 1964, the company is perhaps most famous for its fine audio speakers and headphones, as well as a litigious attitude when it comes to protecting their intellectual property. I know this because my mate got sued by them in the 1990s when he started a streetwear company called POSE – he used the Bose logo, but changed the 'B' to a 'P'. Well naughty.

BOWERS & WILKINS

This loudspeaker and headphone specialist was started in 1966 by John Bowers in the seaside town of Worthing. In 1982 the company created its own audio research centre in the old Scale Model Equipment building (see p190), complete with listening rooms and a semi-anechoic (audio perfect with no reflected sound) studio. An innovative and award-winning company producing consistently excellent products: even content monitor speakers for the BBC, which is really saying something.

BOGEN

The story behind the David Bogen Company is a classic Jewish immigrant, 'rags to riches' tale. In 1909, the talented electronics engineer David Bogen emigrated from Russia to Texas where in 1932 he established his electrical equipment distribution company. After receiving a large order for amplifiers he was unable to find a firm willing to manufacture them – so he decided to tool up and produce them himself. Bogen produced valuable communications technology for the American war effort, and post-war, he was in a great position to capitalise on soaring demand for hi-fi and home audio. An astute businessman, Bogen expanded cleverly, before selling in 1956. The company still thrives today.

Brubeck
plays

BOGEN

STEREO
HIGH FIDELITY
COMPONENTS
1964

BOWERS & WILKINS
Precision Monitor Loudspeakers

electronic

BRINKMAN

This is a brochure for Brinkman Ceramic Speakers showing off their radical 'Open Sound' units. Not the easiest thing to spot – they are the creamic-looking, vase-like creations sitting on the antique furniture. Developed by this British company, their design apparently allowed sound to flow everywhere. As you can see the lady is really enjoying the experience. Not to be confused with the German company Brinkmann who make £20K turntables.

BRAUN

Radio- und Fernsehgeräte im Stile unserer Zeit

BRAUN

Neue Geräte

BRAUN

Triennale 1957
Vitrine der Nationen

Großer internationaler Erfolg

Bei der XI. Triennale in Mailand erhielten alle ausgestellten Braun-Geräte den Grand Prix, die höchste internationale Auszeichnung für gute Industrieform. Die SK-Kleinsuper waren als einziges deutsches Beispiel in die Vitrine der Nationen aufgenommen worden. (Titelbild).

In den Musterwohnungen der Interbau

Bei der Interbau in Berlin waren die Musterwohnungen nur mit technisch hervorragenden und in ihrer Form richtungweisenden Erzeugnissen ausgestattet. Beim Auswählen der Rundfunk- und Fernsehmodelle entschieden sich fast alle Wohnraumgestalter unabhängig voneinander für Braun-Geräte. Mehr als 80 Rundfunk- und Fernsehgeräte von Braun waren in die Interbau aufgenommen.

Musterwohnung mit SK 4
Architekt: Professor E. Ludwig

Stereo High Fidelity
Einführung und Anleitung

BRAUN Stereo High Fidelity
Einführung und Anleitung
4. erweiterte Auflage

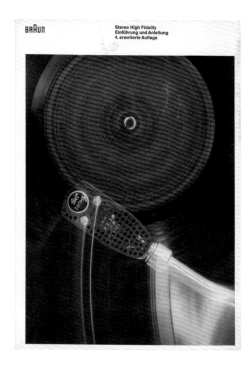

BRAUN TG 60 Hi-Fi Stereo Tape Recorder

BRAUN Lautsprechereinheiten

BRAUN

Lautsprechereinheiten

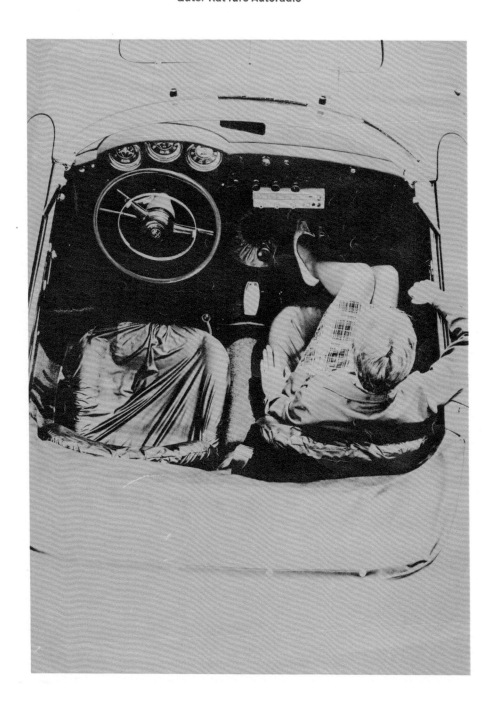

BRAUN

Braun was established in 1921 and by the 1930s was producing exceptional modern technology, including fine and highly regarded high-fidelity audio products such as the groundbreaking radiogram (1932). But things really started to get interesting in the mid-1950s when contemporary concepts of German modernism and industrial design began to combine. In 1955, Dieter Rams joined the company as an architect and interior designer. In 1961 he was appointed head of design, a position he held until 1995. Early (and now classic) audio products developed by him and his team include the SK4, a combined record and radio player (1956, known as 'Snow White's Coffin'), and the T 1000 transistor radio (1963, see below). Some of the brochures shown here, like many of the products they feature, are mythically rare.

BRAUN

1 '74

**Braun High Fidelity
Gesamtkatalog**

**Braun
High**
Fidelity Braun High Fidelity Braun High Fidelity Braun
High
Fidelity

Geräte und Systeme

BRAUN

PS 450
HiFi Plattenspieler

Der PS 450 ist ein automatischer Plattenspieler: Zum Ingangsetzen muß nur ein Schalter betätigt werden, dann schwenkt der Tonarm selbsttätig auf die Platte.

Konstruktionsmerkmale und technische Werte von Laufwerk und Tonarm qualifizieren den PS 450 als Gerät der gehobenen HiFi Klasse.

Zum Bedienungskomfort gehören außer der Automatik eine Drehzahlfeineinstellung und eine Antiskatingeinrichtung, die getrennt für konische und elliptische Nadeln zu justieren ist.

PS 450 ist im Kompaktgerät audio 400 S eingebaut, eine Version ohne Automatik im audio 308 S.

BRAUN

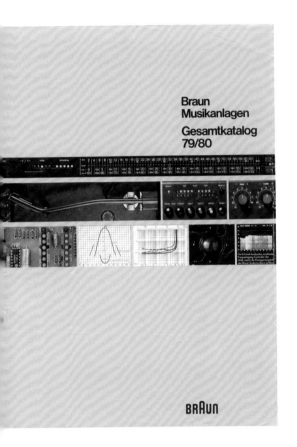

Braun
Musikanlagen

Gesamtkatalog
79/80

BRAUN

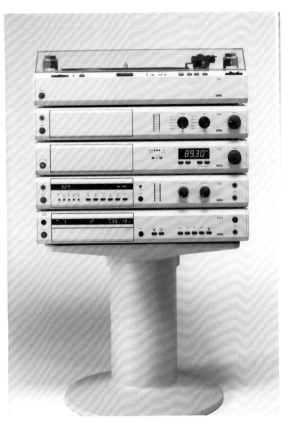

BUSH

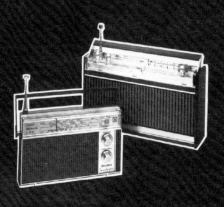

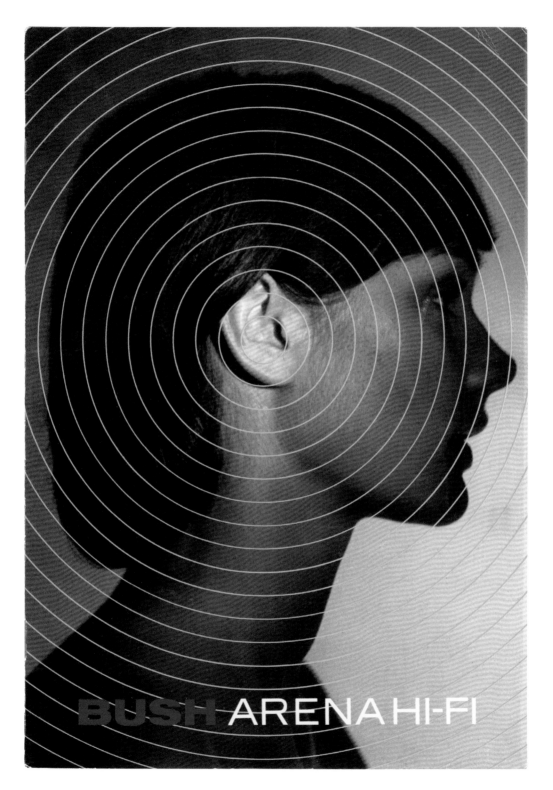

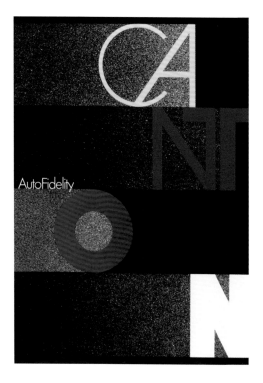

AutoFidelity

BUSH

Bush Radio was founded in 1932, rising from the ashes of an earlier cinematic loudspeaker company originally affiliated to the famous film producer and distributor, Gaumont. The firm was named after Shepherd's Bush, the location of the original studios; however, after early rapid expansion, production was moved to Chiswick. Gobbled up by the Rank empire in 1945, Bush went on to produce some of the most popular and iconic radios of all time. But success brought mergers and disappointing collaborations. Sainsbury's bought the brand in 2016. You can still buy Bush products in Argos.

CANTON

Established in 1972, this German high-end loudspeaker company apparently make good bookshelf speakers.

CBS

This very large record company issued a series of classic cassette tapes and made this brochure which we like – mainly because it shows bikers wearing weird helmets and a groovy cassette player. In the 1970s they also got into quadraphonic releases, which is pretty cool too.

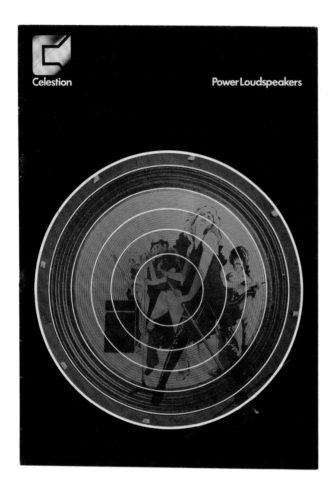

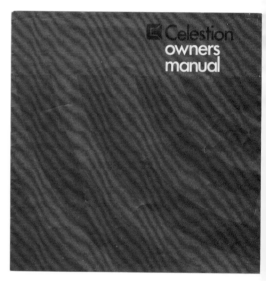

CELESTION

The origins of this company can be traced to 1924 and the early rumblings of broadcasting and sound reproduction. The electrical instrument manufacturing firm, established by Cyril French and his brothers in Hampton Wick, developed a patented in-cabinet speaker constructed from a paper diaphragm and bamboo. Named 'The Celestion', this hugely successful speaker led to the formation of The Celestion Radio Company (1927). Hit hard by the Great Depression of the 1930s, and the restrictions placed upon them during World War II, in 1947 the company was eventually sold to the American firm Rola. In 1992, they were purchased by Kinergetics Holdings (no, I have no idea who they are either). Some of the mid-1970s brochures are a bit *Abigail's Party*.

celestion
international

celestion
international

Get it on

Dansette

cp the sound sellers!

Musique

The same specification as Musique
de Luxe but styled in padded black
leathercloth cabinet with teak lid.
Legs optional extra.

39 gns. TAX PAID

DANSETTE

1952 saw the birth of the Dansette record player
(manufactured by J.A. Margolin Ltd). The timing was near
perfect – the birth of pop was just around the corner and
within a few years teens throughout the country were
loading up Dansettes with their newly bought singles and
LPs. These were functional, portable machines, perfect for
teen parties and complete with an autochanger, allowing
you to stack the player high with singles that it would then
play in turn. By the late 1960s technology and taste had
moved on, but the Dansette has become a byword for the
portable record player, and the importance of this icon in
the development of rock and pop is assured.

DBX

Started by David E. Blackmer in 1971, dbx are leaders in
live audio reproduction. The name is derived from one of
their early products, the e**X**panded range **D**eci**B**el meter.

Popular 12½ gns. TAX PAID   **Viva** 17 gns. TAX PAID

A light easily portable unit with a quality of reproduction which would
do credit to many a larger record player.
⊕ Independent tone and volume controls ⊕ Latest non-automatic,
4-speed B.S.R. unit ⊕ Plays all sizes of records ⊕ 5" loudspeaker
Size: 12½"×10½"×6½". Weight: 8½ lbs.

All Dansette's fine features of styling and sound at a competitive price.
⊕ Latest autochange unit ⊕ Takes all records with the lid closed
⊕ Independent on/off volume and tone controls ⊕ Universal stand
available
Size: 17"×16"×7". Weight: 16½ lbs.

the sound of silence
professional noise reduction system for the small recording studio

DECIBEL

This short-lived Italian company made a small series of 'cigarette butt' style surround-sound speakers. Yes, they actually look like cigarette butts – to me at least – which is why I've called them that (see if you can spot them in the photograph above).

DTR Research Corporation
Design Speaker Series

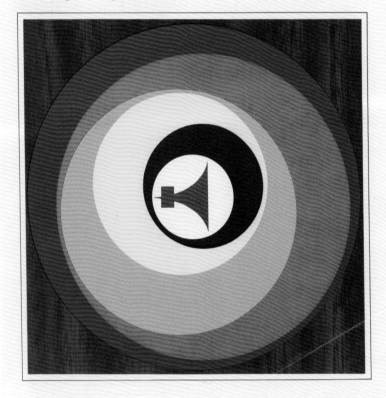

DTR

This small company was established by engineer Arnold Takemoto whose dream it was to create a revolutionary futuristic design for speakers that would give 'the ultimate in sound reproduction'. I think this was in the early 1970s, I'm fairly certain he was unsuccessful.

DIATONE

The loudspeaker division of Japanese giant Mitsubishi began manufacturing monitors for broadcasting in 1945. It appears that, in later life, they piggy-backed inventive technological ideas and made their own versions – like this bonkers linear turntable, which people would now kill for.

DIATONE®

音楽が、生活のメニューをおいしくします。デッキレシーバーとプレーヤーが一体となって、
ステレオをさらに身近にしたダイヤトーン・セットアップコンポX-10形。

ダイヤトーン・セットアップコンポ

Setup Compo X-10

Dual
Stereo-Components

Dual-Programm
1970/71

Plattenspieler-, Automatikspieler-,
Hi-Fi-Automatikspieler-Chassis

27

DUAL

In 1907, the Steidinger brothers started to manufacture gramophone player parts in the town of St Georgen in the Black Forest – home of the cuckoo clock and historically a place where people tinker with all things clockwork. In 1927 they developed the Dual-Motor: a groundbreaking half-clockwork, half-electric gramophone motor. This invention was followed by the Dual turntable (1935), a product so popular that after World War II, Dual became the largest manufacturer of turntables in Europe. They continued to be successful and inventive in the audio market until the 1970s, when a tsunami of cheap Japanese technology smashed everything apart. After it went bankrupt in 1982, the company was sold to a French manufacturer.

Stereo-Heimanlagen, Hi-Fi-Kompakt-Anlagen

Stereo-Componenten, Hi-Fi-Stereo-Componenten

Phonokoffer, Heimgerät, Stereo-Phonokoffer

This is an entertainer...

It's a new breed! A completely portable component music system. We call it **ENTERTAINER I**, and it **is** entertainment at its best. The amplifier-turntable and two speaker modules deliver thrillingly faithful sound reproduction.

How was it done? First we developed a unique solid-state circuit to take full advantage of modern high quality transistors. Result—a clean, cool thirty watts of concert-quality sound. Then we added famous E-V loudspeakers, like those used in component systems, in acoustically correct molded enclosures. You get no less than faithful reproduction over an extremely wide range.

We installed a *Garrard* automatic turntable—the standard of the high fidelity field. Plays all standard records, up to eight automatically. Then we built in our own E-V ultra-linear ceramic stereo cartridge. To top it off, the diamond turnover stylus is performance-guaranteed for the life of your **ENTERTAINER**.

All of this high fidelity with a handle is wrapped up in handsome molded Terra-brown cases that can't fade, chip, scuff, or peel. It goes anywhere with you.

Why not hear it? You'll be sold by the sound. **ENTERTAINER I** is for you.

Form No. 1020   Litho in U.S.A.

ELECTRO VOICE

This American company began in 1927 servicing radio receivers. The Great Depression led to insolvency, but their fortunes turned around after the founders decided to focus on audio products. They designed a public address system for the legendary Notre Dame college football coach, Knute Rockne, who had struggled to be heard at training sessions due to ill health. Rockne dubbed the system his 'Electro Voice' and the name stuck. Over the following decades EV developed noise-cancelling microphones (initially for communications during fighting in World War II), turntable pick-up cartridges and the first commercial quadraphonic system. They also made the groovy portable 'Entertainer' deck shown here, with help from Garrard (see p86). The company still survives today as a subsidiary of Bosch.

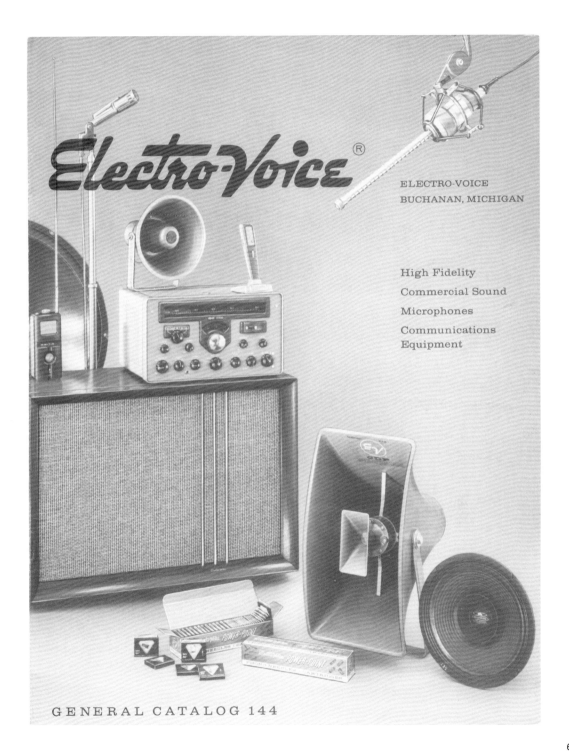

Electro-Voice ®

ELECTRO-VOICE
BUCHANAN, MICHIGAN

High Fidelity
Commercial Sound
Microphones
Communications
Equipment

GENERAL CATALOG 144

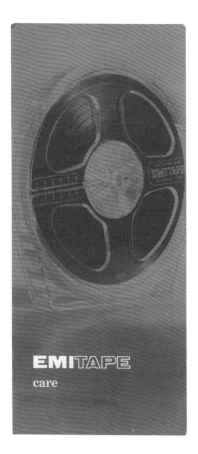

EMITAPE

care

Adding sound
to slides with
EMITAPE

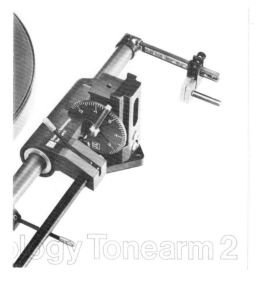

Eminent Technology Tonearm 2

EMITAPE for
home movies

EMITAPE
for parties

EMINENT TECHNOLOGY

Founded in 1982 by Bruce Thigpen, this company is still active today. Their first manufactured product was an airbearing phonograph tonearm named the Model 1. Focussing on research and development, their history is full of interesting technology such as flat speakers, planar tweeters and rotary-fan woofers.

EMI

Yes, we all know about EMI. Here are some great brochures they made for their tape range. The company manufactured both amateur and professional-level tape, from the mid-1950s onwards. EMI high-grade tape played an important part in the history of modern music – such was its quality that the Beatles used it to record all their studio work.

EMT

Short for Elektromesstechnik, EMT was founded in Berlin in 1938 by Wilhelm Franz. In 1943, as Allied bombing intensified, they moved out of the city, eventually ending up in Southern Germany. Their first turntable was constructed in 1951; this beast could play 16" transcription discs and was equipped with a strobe, to fine tune revolution speed. Their subsequent unrivalled turntables developed and adapted the pioneering technology of the time, such as stereo sound, to become the default turntables of broadcasters (and now hi-fi geeks) around the world. EMT also produced the 140 Reverberation Unit in 1957, four of which were immediately installed at Abbey Road (they ended up with a total of seven). EMT was bought by a Belgian company in 1989 and audio equipment production was gradually phased out.

EPI

The company was founded in 1970 by Winslow Burhoe, who had developed a unique woofer to tweeter ratio, which he incorporated into a set of speakers. For the next two decades, EPI continued to design new products, but sonic rumour has it that nothing quite matched up to the early 'Brown Booklet' models, as depicted on the cover of the brown booklet shown above.

EMPIRE SCIENTIFIC

This successful, low-budget stylus maker is now owned by Russell Industries. They no longer advertise using ladies' legs and golden stilettos.

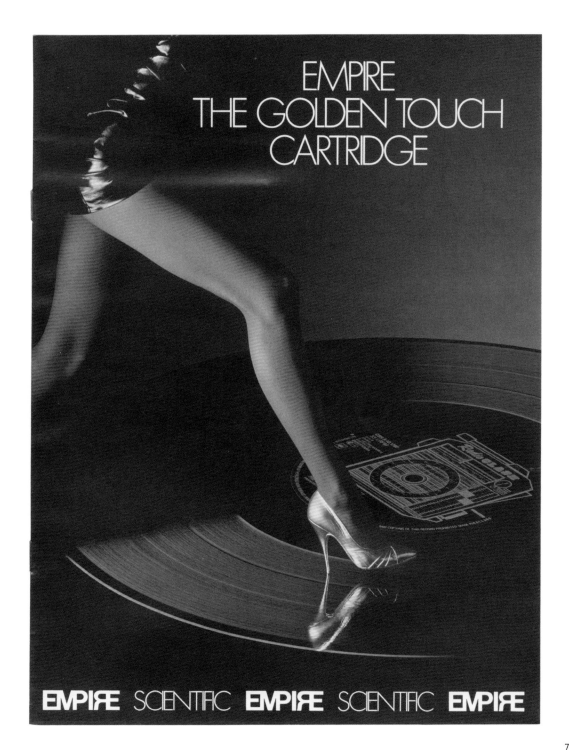

EMPIRE
THE GOLDEN TOUCH
CARTRIDGE

EMPIRE SCIENTIFIC EMPIRE SCIENTIFIC EMPIRE

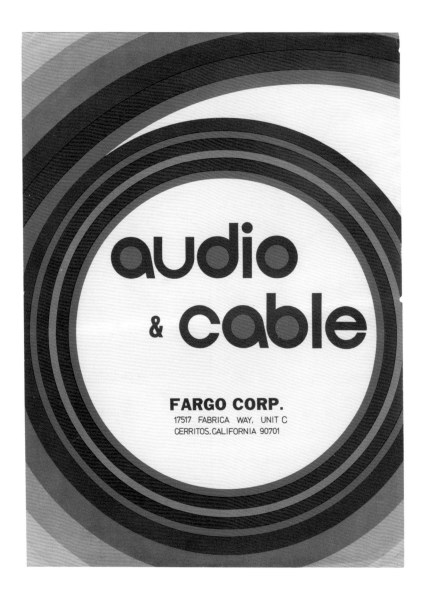

audio & cable

FARGO CORP.

17517 FABRICA WAY, UNIT C
CERRITOS, CALIFORNIA 90701

FARGO CORP

I wasn't expecting a company that made speaker cables back in the 1970s to become one of the largest international industrial cable manufacturers ever, but that's what happened. They still produce cables for speakers, alongside underground stuff, pylons and just about everything else.

FAIRFAX

This New Jersey company made high-quality speakers, often with complex grille work. I can find very little up to date information about them, so it's likely their plug has been pulled.

nel silenzio un'amica, la filodiffusione

FERGUSON

Before World War II, the American-Canadian electronics company manufactured commercial products for the UK based on successful American designs. They became part of the British Radio Corp, eventually being taken over by Thorn in the late 1950s. Ferguson produced affordable and desirable products that proved hugely popular for decades. In the 1980s, facing heavy competition from Japanese imports, the company was sold.

FILODIFFUSIONE

This is basically cable radio in Italy – and this is a groovy booklet promoting it. Just look at how great everyone looks and how much fun they're having when they are listening to cable radio.

FISHER

Keen violinist Avery Fisher started his New York radio company back in 1945. They quickly became known for producing pioneering, high-performance audio products, possibly the first to manufacture separate – but matched – audio components. The successful company was bought and sold, eventually ending up as part of Sanyo in 1975.

FISHER SPEAKER SYSTEMS

High-Efficiency, High-Compliance Sound Reproducers for the Home

Compacts · Book Shelf · Slim-Line · Consolette Floor Models · Accessories

Fisher

Stereo

Components

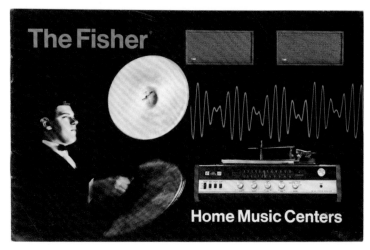

FISHER RADIO CORPORATION · LONG ISLAND CITY 1, N. Y.

The Natural
Sound
of Fisher
Components

GALE

Ira Gale started making speakers in the early 1970s. This power-hungry product was notable for its futuristic design and ability to handle very high sound levels. It appears the company is still going, but whoever runs the website is deaf to my emails.

GS401A Loudspeaker

Photography Berris Conolly

GARRARD

The Garrard Engineering and Manufacturing Company was founded in Swindon, in 1915, by the jewellery company of the same name. Garrard went on to become (arguably) the best British turntable manufacturer, producing a series of mechanically perfect transcription turntables, which played at all speeds and were ideal for broadcast use. By the late 1970s it all got a bit messy business wise, but the good news is SME (see p190) took ownership of the brand in 2018 and Garrard Turntables UK Ltd are back in business.

Garrard multiple play automatic turntables

The Music Recovery Module from Garrard.

An essential component for every music system.

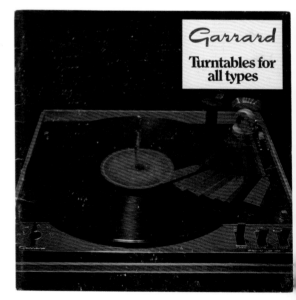

Garrard Turntables for all types

Model 401

When only the best will do, when only perfection is permissible, broadcaster and connoisseur alike turn to the Garrard 401 transcription turntable. For they know that when they buy the 401 they are buying the finest example of transcription turntable technology available.

Styled by one of Britain's leading designers, the 401 combines elegance with craftsman engineering. Metallescent charcoal and chrome relief echo its superb performance.

The heart of the 401 is a high and low-voltage range (110 to 125V and 220 to 250V) shaded-pole induction motor (Fig. 1). This is mounted on six specially tensioned springs which act as an extremely effective vibration barrier. Surrounding the motor is a heavy iron case which ensures full magnetic screening, while a fully suppressed double-pole switch controls its mains supply.

The 401 operates at three standard speeds—33⅓, 45 and 78 rev/min. Around the periphery of the turntable are accurately spaced stroboscopic markings and these are illuminated by a high-intensity neon lamp inset in the rigid base. This is a unique feature of the 401 enabling a visual check of the turntable speed. If adjustment is needed there is a conveniently situated control on the front panel of the unit permitting the speed to be varied by plus or minus 3 per cent (Fig 2).

The balanced, machined turntable is an aluminium, gravity casting weighing approximately six pounds. Each unit undergoes the most rigorous inspection and test before it leaves our factory. And the final performance figures are recorded and enclosed with the unit.

Size: 13¾ in (349 mm) wide by 14⅝ in (371 mm) front to rear by 2⅛ in (54 mm) above and 3⅞ in (100 mm) below lower edge of unit plate. Space must be allowed to accommodate chosen pickup arm.

Performance
Wow and flutter better than 0·08% r.m.s.
Rumble (relative to 1·4 cm/sec @ 100Hz)
better than −51dB.

GEC
SOBELL

the Wonderful World of Sight & Sound

Stardeck C.R. 200

Stardeck C.S 560

Stardeck

Model A1-400

12-inch Dual-Coaxial High Fidelity Speaker

GE Custom Music Ensemble

GENERAL GE ELECTRIC

GEC
makes a
world of difference
to your home...

GEC

The General Electric Company was a major UK-based conglomerate. Founded in 1886 as an electronics wholesaler, the company invested heavily in electric lighting, which proved very profitable. During the World Wars they supplied products to the armed forces, as well as helping develop military technology, such as radar. Postwar expansion meant that by 1980, GEC was the largest employer in Britain with over 250,000 employees. Over this period they produced some decent audio gear, from early kit-based speakers to standard hi-fi and cash-in home entertainment fare. Hugely successful across many electronic avenues, in 1984 the company was one of the first to feature in the newly formed FTSE 100 Index. In the late 1990s parts of GEC were sold off and in 1998 the final element (mainly telecommunications) amalgamated with other firms to form Marconi Communications.

GOLDRING

Established in 1906, this German electronics company relocated from Berlin to England in 1933. Famed for making functional gramophones, turntables and eventually moving coil cartridges. A family business until 1987, they're still sounding good over a century later – and now produce pretty fine headphones too.

GOODMANS

This London-based company began manufacturing public address systems and loudspeakers in 1923. They have forged a great reputation for fine speakers and amplifiers and still produce quality modern audio equipment.

GRUNDIG

Grundig started life in 1945 as a German electronics shop. Initially producing radios in kit form (to bypass post-war restrictions), in 1951 they began to manufacture television sets and portable tape recorders. In 1960, they opened a plant in Belfast to produce tape recorders. In 1973, during the Troubles, the Provisional IRA kidnapped the managing director of the factory, Thomas Niedermayer. Secret negotiations were held with the British government, but these were abruptly ended by the IRA. In 1980, Niedermayer's body was found in a shallow grave. After recovering from such a shock, the company continued to expand into different areas of fashionable technology, eventually declaring insolvency in 2003, after lines of credit had been exhausted. They were purchased by the Turkish company Koç Holdings in 2007 and still produce an enormous range of electronic grey, white and silver goods.

THE TK 46

First choice for professionals who know and amateurs who care. A very advanced, very remarkable four-track full stereo/mono machine. Separate recording, playback and erase heads and separate recording, playback amplifiers, with superimposition facilities on all four tracks mean that the horizons of the TK 46 owner are limitless. There are facilities, too, for multiple synchronization, monitoring via tape and the recording of echoes.

The brilliant TK 46 has 2 output stages and loudspeakers giving a total output power of 7 watts. This truly is the Grundig man's Grundig.

99 GUINEAS (STEREO OR MONO MICROPHONE EXTRA)

The matchless and brilliant TK 40, 41 and 46 are part of the wide range of Grundig tape recorders—the biggest range in the world. Remember too, that Grundig make the world's finest radios, radiograms and dictating machines. Ask your dealer for a demonstration of the TK 40, 41, 46 or any Grundig model that suits your purpose. There's bound to be one that does, and the easiest H.P. terms are always available.

sound in action—Grundig

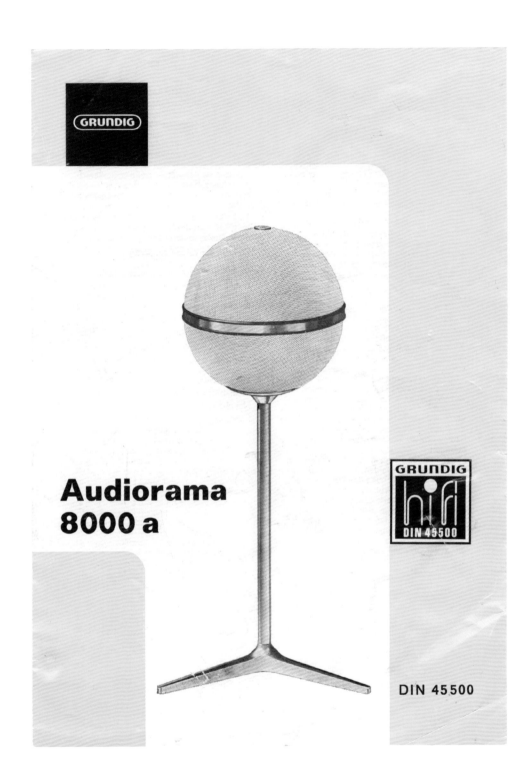

GRUNDIG

**Audiorama
8000 a**

GRUNDIG
hifi
DIN 45500

DIN 45500

Tracking Force:	0°
Skating Force:	0
Tone Arm Mass (effective):	6 gms
Stylus Overhang:	0
Turntable Rumble DIN B..:	–57 dB
Wow and Flutter NAB weighted:	0.045%
Hum (Tone Arm In) DIN 45544::	–70 dB
Speeds:	33⅓, 45 RPM
Speed Constancy:	±0.3%
Motor/Drive:	Synchronous AC with precision ground belt
Platter Weight:	2.4 lbs (1.1 kg)
Dimensions (incl. dust cover):	6¾"H x 16½"W x 16¼"D 171mm H x 419mm W x 413mm D
Weight Total:	20 lbs (9.1 kg)

harman/kardon

55 Ames Court, Plainview, N.Y. 11803
Printed in U.S.A.
All specifications and features are
subject to change without notice

6/79

harman/kardon   **HK2000**
stereo cassette deck

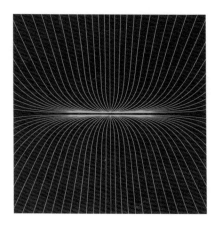

HARMAN/KARDON

This American company was founded by Sidney Harman and Bernard Kardon in Westbury, New York, in 1953. Kardon had worked for the audio electronics company David Bogen (see p38) during during the war, where he produced underwater acoustic equipment, as well as developing methods of silent communication and brilliant sonic deception. He formed Harman/Kardon when he realised the potential of the new domestic audio market, something that Bogen had chosen to ignore at the time. Within a few years the company had become extremely successful, but Kardon left in 1959 to pursue a career in ultrasound dentistry equipment. Harman continued to build the company across a broad range of audio appliances, and although the corporate story is complicated (it is currently owned by Samsung), they still manufacture audio equipment. In 2000, they collaborated with Apple to produce the Harman Kardon SoundSticks, which were hugely popular at the time, but look a bit dated now.

HILL-CRAFT

This California-based company began building beautiful hi-fi cabinets in the late 1950s.

harman/kardon

sound-engineered

STEREO FURNITURE

by master cabinet makers

HILL-CRAFT

as beautiful as the sound it produces

HILL-CRAFT MFG. CO.

14621 South Hindry Avenue
Lawndale, California
ORegon 8-8078

BULLETIN No. 661

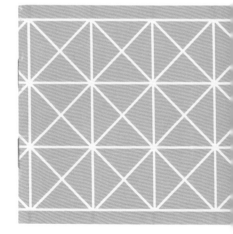

HITACHI

The Japanese technology giant was established in 1910, as the electrical arm of a mining operation based in the city of Hitachi. The most interesting non-corporate fact I could find was that the firm's toponymic name derives from two Kanji characters: *Hi* meaning 'Sun', and *Tachi* meaning 'Rise'.

HITACHI

Audio to suit every mood

Volume 2 1976/77

SOUND

...better buy Hitachi.

◎ HITACHI

**MODEL 418
PHOTO CUBE RADIO**

Features:
- AM Radio
- Holds 4 Pictures Up to 3¼"
  Square
- Comes Complete with 9 V Battery

Color   4 Assorted Colors:
Light Green, Navy Blue
Mustard Yellow and Coral

ICP

**MODEL 931
PANDA RADIO**

Features:
- AM Radio
- Panda Figure with Carrying
  Strap
- Complete with Battery
  (9V006P) 1 PC.
- Instructions
- Booklet and Guarantee Card
- Printed Gift Box

Colors   Black and White Only

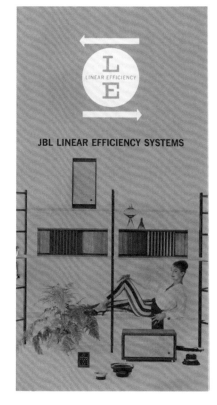

JBL LINEAR EFFICIENCY SYSTEMS

ICP

This has been in my collection for some time, mainly because of the teddy/panda radio. I thought they were manufacturers of novelty radios (there is a 'Twister'-based radio in this leaflet too). However, it turns out this is a sales brochure for The International Centre of Photography, in New York.

JBL

AGENT GÉNÉRAL:
AURIEMA - FRANCE
92-98, Bd Victor-Hugo
92 - CLICHY
Tél: 270.80.30

James B. Lansing Sound, Inc., 3249 Casitas Avenue, Los Angeles, California 90039, U.S.A.

JBL

This Los Angeles company, specialising in superior speaker systems related to the cinema, was established as Lansing Manufacturing in 1927 by James Bullough Lansing and his business partner Ken Decker. In 1939, Decker died in an airplane crash. The financial problems that followed led to the company being bought by the Altec Service Coporation and renamed Altec Lansing (see p21). When his contract expired in 1946, Lansing left the company to form James B. Lansing Sound (JBL). Their first product, the D175 high-frequency driver, was launched in the same year and remained in production until the mid-1970s. Sadly James Lansing committed suicide in 1949 (possibly due to mounting bills and business-related stress). Under the control of vice president Bill Thomas, JBL experienced a long period of strong growth and innovation, with some speakers remaining in production and on catalogue for decades. In the 1970s the company became a household name in America, dominating both the professional and domestic markets with sublime speakers such as the L100 – which incidentally are being manufactured again. JBL is currently owned by Harman International Industries, part of the giant they call Samsung.

The JBL Limited

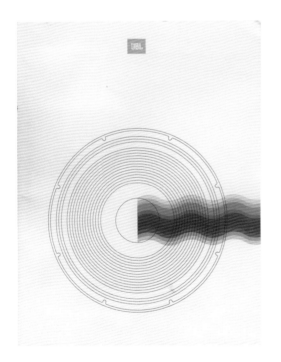

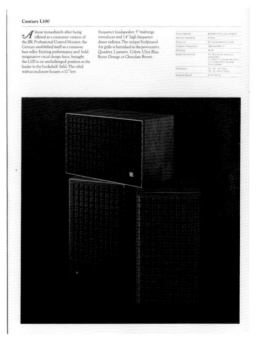

Century L100

*A*lmost immediately after being offered as a consumer version of the JBL Professional Control Monitor, the Century established itself as a runaway best seller. Exciting performance and bold, imaginative visual design have brought the L100 to an unchallenged position as the leader in the bookshelf field. The oiled walnut enclosure houses a 12" low frequency loudspeaker, 5" midrange transducer and 1.4" high frequency direct radiator. The unique Sculptured Air grille is furnished in the provocative Quadrex 2 pattern. Colors: Ultra Blue, Burnt Orange or Chocolate Brown.

Power Capacity	50 Watts RMS continuous program
Nominal Impedance	8 ohms
Crossover	10" composite and unique
Crossover Frequencies	1500 and 4000 Hz
Efficiency	90 dB
System Components	12" TL (low) see frequency loudspeaker, 2 (10cm) 5" Direct Radiator, 1.4" (4 cm) HIGH Frequency Direct radiator
Dimensions	14" x 24" x 14" deep, 7/8 = 24 x 36 x 34 (actual)
Shipped Weight	38 lbs (19 kg)

JVC

The Japan Victor Company. The big boys. Established in 1927 as part of the Victor Talking Machine Company, which was subsequently bought by the Radio Corporation of America (RCA). Initially producing phonographs and records, then later radios and early television sets. In 1943, with World War II raging, they split from RCA, but kept rights to the 'Victor' and 'His Master's Voice' trademarks in Japan. In 1953, JVC became part of Panasonic. They established a subsidiary in 1963, called JVC Nivico (Nippon Victor Corporation), that produced some highly original and truly groundbreaking technology, such as: the Videosphere; the first discrete four-channel audio system; the first radio with a built-in television; the VHS format; and more. The brand also sponsored Arsenal for two decades. JVC (and its subsidiaries) are still part of the acoustic landscape.

JÜRG JECKLIN

The 'JJ Float', or rather the 'Jürg Jecklin Float' electrostatic headphone, was invented by the eponnymous Swiss sound engineer in 1971. Included in the industrial design collection of the Museum of Modern Art, New York, they have to be the strangest headphones ever. Non adjustable, boxy, odd, but apparently amazingly transparent and dynamic if they fit you and you don't mind looking like a wally.

HOME ENTERTAINMENT CATALOG

JVC

RADIO CASSETTE RECORDERS
For Your Leisure and Pleasure

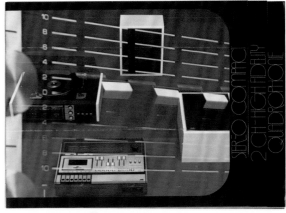

The world of JVC NIVICO

8805
Solid State FM/AM Table Radio with Convertible Top Panel.
One of the most imaginative ideas ever developed in the radio field. The quick change top panel can reflect the real you . . . match your mood. Gives a wholly new appearance. It's almost like owning two radios. Includes at earphone, large 3-inch speaker with exceptionally good tone quality and a big power output far beyond what you'd expect in a unit this size. Also, built-in FM AFC (locks in even distant stations), handsome illuminated dial and easy to use sliding controls. 10 transistors, 11 diodes.
3-1/2"H x 10"W x 10"D. 4.6 lbs.

Chessmen not included

HIGH FIDELITY CATALOG

JVC

VIDEOSPHERE

3240
Videosphere A 9-inch Diagonal (38 sq. in.) All-Purpose Portable.

Capable of being rotated to any angle, the 3240 represents the finest in advanced JVC technology and design. Highly innovative, it is the epitome of convenience, ready for instant viewing indoors or out. No more of the tiring neck-craning that is a built-in liability with fixed-position television sets. You adjust the 3240 to the position that suits you best, whether you're sitting up, lying down or doing some household or office chore. Lightweight, and of a unique globular shape, the 3240 offers both VHF and UHF reception, and features instant-start picture, a discreet no-glare screen, a built-in rod antenna and an earphone jack. AC/DC. The new JVC 3240. Videosphere. In red-orange, ivory or black. 25 transistors, 17 diodes.
11-1/4" Diameter. 2-15/16"H x 7-3/16"W x 7-3/16"D (Base). 11.5lbs.

3241
Videosphere A 9-inch Diagonal (38 sq. in.) All-Purpose Portable with Digital Clock.

The JVC 3240 offers even more versatility as the JVC 3241, a model mounted on a special swivel base for 360° rotation. This base is complete with a built-in digital clock that features an alarm buzzer, an up-to-three-hour Sleep Timer and an automatic TV shut-off device.
11-1/4" Diameter. 3-23/32"H x 7-31/64"W x 7-11/16"D (Base). 11.6 lbs.

3240

JVC Home Entertainment Catalogue

JVC High Fidelity Catalogue

CONTENTS:

NIVICO
VICTOR COMPANY OF JAPAN, LTD.
TOKYO, JAPAN

KENWOOD presents with pride its complete new line of stereo components: Receivers, Amplifiers, Tuners, Tape Decks, Compacts, Cassette Deck, and Speaker Systems. For the highest fidelity in sound reproduction... for superb craftsmanship and unexcelled stereo engineering... for custom design with the look and feel of luxury, choose KENWOOD and enjoy stereo listening at its trouble-free best.

KENWOOD

This Japanese consumer electronics brand began life in 1946 as The Kasuga Radio Company, producing amateur radio equipment. Renamed Trio Coporation in 1960, the firm grew and expanded globally, selling radio and hi-fi equipment. The brand Kenwood was established as the exclusive importer of Trio products into America. The name is an amalgamation of 'Ken' – a name common in both Japan and America, and 'Wood' – a reliable material, but also a reference to Hollywood: a combination that they believed would work well in the market. Eventually Kenwood products outsold those of Trio; consequently the company rebranded itself as Kenwood in 1986. In 2007 they merged with JVC and JVCKenwood was born. Excuse me if I have this history a bit wrong, but it's one of the most complex stories about a hi-fi company I've ever come across.

KENWOOD
TOP HIFI

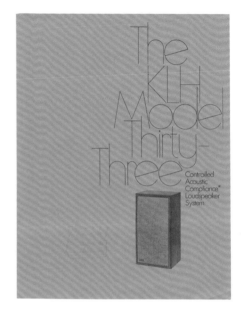

KLH

Founders Henry Kloss, Malcolm S. Low and Joseph Anton Hoffman established the KLH Research and Development Corporation in 1957. From their small base in Cambridge, Massachusetts, they briefly became the largest loudspeaker company in the world. Specialising in superior high-fidelity reproduction, audiophile-quality speakers, KLH released several groundbreaking models. The company was sold to David Kelly of Klipsch and Voxx fame and still thrives today.

LEAR JET

That's right – this is related to the company that makes private jets. Founder Bill Lear was an interesting all-round inventor, involved in projects encompassing batteries, in-car stereos and aviation. To cut a long-ish story short, Lear was part of a consortium that invented the eight-track cartridge. In 1963 an employee of Lear, Richard Kraus, developed the Lear Jet Stereo 8 Tape Cartridge. In addition, by simplifying the internal parts, he dramatically increased their playing time. With home, car and portable versions, they became a hugely popular format.

LOEWE OPTA

Founded in 1923 by bothers Siegmund and David Loewe, this German company presented the first fully electronic television at the 1931 Berlin Radio Show. When Hitler came to power, Siegmund Loewe emigrated to America. He returned in 1949 to produce the Optaphon, a cassette tape recorder, and later the Optacord 500, a video recorder (1961). After his death in 1962, the company ceased to be a family concern and is currently owned by Skytec Group Ltd. I'm not sure how long they made the laundry basket hi-fi shown here, but I doubt it was a bestseller.

LOWTHER

In 1926, Paul Voight (born in England to German parents) built the UK's first electronic recording system. He teamed up with Lowther Manufacturing in 1936 to produce luxury radios and speakers. In 1953, suffering ill health and tired of post-war anti-German sentiment, Voight emigrated to Canada, leaving chief engineer Donald Chave to run the company. Lowther continue to innovate and still produce some of the finest handmade speakers available to man.

Lear Jet
Stereo 8

→ for people
→ on the
→ Go

LOEWE OPTA

Stereo-Box 3820 W

~towards perfection~

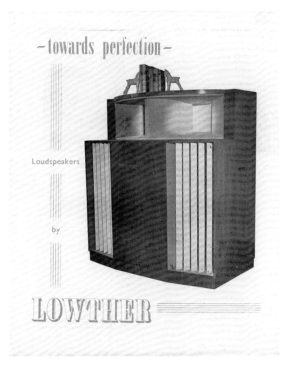

Loudspeakers

by

LOWTHER

HI-FI SOUND SYSTEM
L&G

Looking Good, Sounding Better

Old-man brown and spinster-black are out! No longer the sophisticated old component sitting sedately on the shelf. L & G gives liberated vitality in modern design and performance, bringing a fresher, brighter appearance to high-fidelity.

New colour concepts in controls and cabinets. Geometrical front panels for symmetrical unit trinity or single unit harmony.

In electronic theory and internal construction, these hi-fi youngsters carry on the heritage of the past masters, but with the refinements of recent technology and the vivacity of modern art.

L & G stereo equipment assures top quality reproduced sound to give listening pleasure to all ages—from innovative youth to the discriminating fuddy-dud. Come along in a whirl of living fun at a moderate price!

Come Wrap the Sounds Around You

L&G

This small brand, created in 1972, is an offshoot from Luxman, the prestigious Japanese audio company. L&G produced fashionable and very colourful stereos for the modern way of life. Obviously they didn't want any of this fun diluting their own brand of serious stereo technology.

KOSS

This Milwaukee company was established in 1953 by John C. Koss as a television rental company. Koss introduced the first high-fidelity stereo headphones in 1958. He came across the idea of headphones by accident, while working alongside engineer Martin Lange, trying to develop a portable phonograph with a privacy switch feature – previously, headphones had only ever been used in connection with communications. Koss soon came to dominate the domestic headphone market. The rest of the company history is colourful and complex, involving bankruptcy, wire fraud, embezzlement, lawsuits and a fortune based on the Gamestop Short Squeeze.

KÖRTING SOUND

Körting Radio Works have origins that go back to a lighting company in Leipzig, founded in 1889. From 1925 onwards the firm made high-quality domestic audio appliances under the Körting brand, as well as being pioneers in colour television. The lights went off in 1978.

MAGNEPLANAR®: Sound + Decor

MAGNEPAN

The company name is Magnepan, the speakers are called Magneplanars and, among enthusiasts, go by the colloquial name of 'Maggies'. Conceived by engineer Jim Whiney, they have been manufactured in Minnesota since 1969. They are super high-end and the technology behind them is weighty and flat: I'm not even going to try to explain any more, suffice to say, the speakers are unrivalled for their sense of sonic space and realism. You can still buy them today.

McINTOSH

The Grateful Dead used McIntosh amplification for their legendary 'Wall Of Sound' stage show. McIntosh powered the sound at Woodstock in 1969. DJ Kool Herc, pioneer of hip hop, used one between his two Technics turntables at block parties. In terms of pure sonic amplification, it gets no better. This American company, founded 1949 by Frank McIntosh and Gordon Gow, specialised in tube amplification for private and industrial use. Vintage McIntosh amplifiers are highly sought after for their warm and lively reproduction.

McIntosh

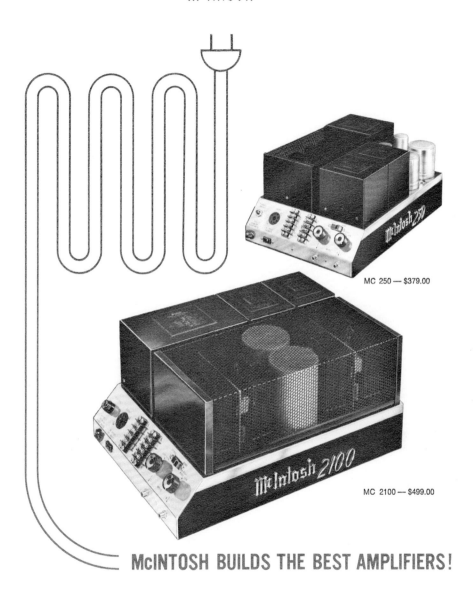

MC 250 — $379.00

MC 2100 — $499.00

McINTOSH BUILDS THE BEST AMPLIFIERS!

MARANTZ

In 1952, Saul Marantz started his high-end audio business from his home in Kew Gardens, New York. The company developed a range of classic amplifiers and hi-fi systems. These influential products reached the height of their success in the 1970s. In the 1980s, after being sold to Philips, the company successfully focussed on compact disc technology, to the detriment of the rest of their range. The firm is currently owned by Sound United LLC (who are not a football club).

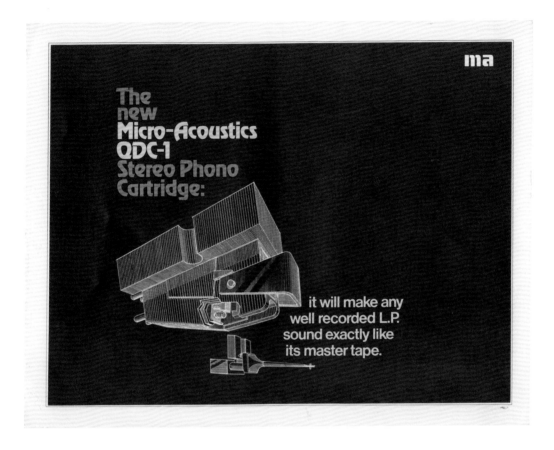

The new Micro-Acoustics QDC-1 Stereo Phono Cartridge:

it will make any well recorded L.P. sound exactly like its master tape.

ma

MEMOREX

Formed in Silicon Valley in 1961, Memorex began life manufacturing computer tape. The name is a portmanteau of 'memory' and 'excellence'. After expanding into all areas of the burgeoning computer world, they entered the human world in 1971 with their now classic advertising campaign 'Is it live or is it Memorex?' The commercial featured jazz legend Ella Fitzgerald singing a note that shatters a glass. The note, recorded onto a Memorex cassette, continues to shatter glass when played back. A nightmare situation in a pub. The company was broken up in 1996 and is now owned by Digital Products International.

MICRO-ACOUSTICS

These late 1960s American, geeky stylus manufacturers specialised in ceramic cartridges, developing and patenting a construction where the stylus arm was directly connected to the ceramic elements. They also made test records for their products – 'one side contains a remarkable series of electronic and musical tests, while the other side is pure music, for sheer enjoyment' – and even held 'stylus clinics' in stockists' showrooms.

J A MICHELL
ENGINEERING
LIMITED

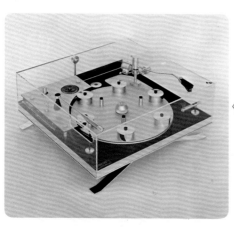

Reference
◄ Hydraulic
Turntable

Fluid Arm

Reference

Hydraulic or Electronic speed control

J A Michell Engineering Ltd

2 Theobald Street · Borehamwood · Hertfordshire · England.
Telephone 01-953 0771/2
Designed & Printed by Bradleys, Reading & London

J.A. MICHELL ENGINEERING

The company, originally based in Borehamwood, has been manufacturing exceptional analogue products since 1973. They also produced the Transcriptors Hydraulic Reference Turntable – arguably the world's most famous turntable – as used in Stanley Kubrick's *A Clockwork Orange* (1971). Originally designed and built by David Gammon in the late 1960s for his own company called Transcriptors, Gammon used the neighbouring engineering company, owned by John Michell, to machine parts for him. It is likely that Michell constructed the Transcriptors made for Kubrick.

In 1973, when Gammon moved production to Ireland, he granted a licence to Michell that allowed him to produce the Hydraulic Reference Turntable under his own name. In 1977 Gammon revoked the licence. Legend has it that during the making of *The Empire Strikes Back*, the *Star Wars* design team – who were based near the Michell headquarters – raided the factory for the Boba Fett costume, using parts of the Transcriptor dust brush for Fett's rocket-propelled kneepad darts. Michell Engineering still thrive and kindly lent us their very rare brochures.

MITSUBISHI

The Mitsubishi Electric Corporation was established in Tokyo in 1921 as an offshoot of the electrical machinery element of Mitsubishi Shipbuilding. The company came to prominence in the audio sector after World War II, mainly through the production of speakers under their Diatone brand name (see p62). This giant global behemoth has applied the power of technology to develop a huge range of products – from electric fans to nuclear power generators, via satellites and workspace robots. In the light of this, their corporate slogan 'Advanced and ever advancing' (used in 1969–2001) sounds more than a little sinister.

MISSION

English manufacturer of fine speakers. But what Stonehenge has to do with it we really do not know.

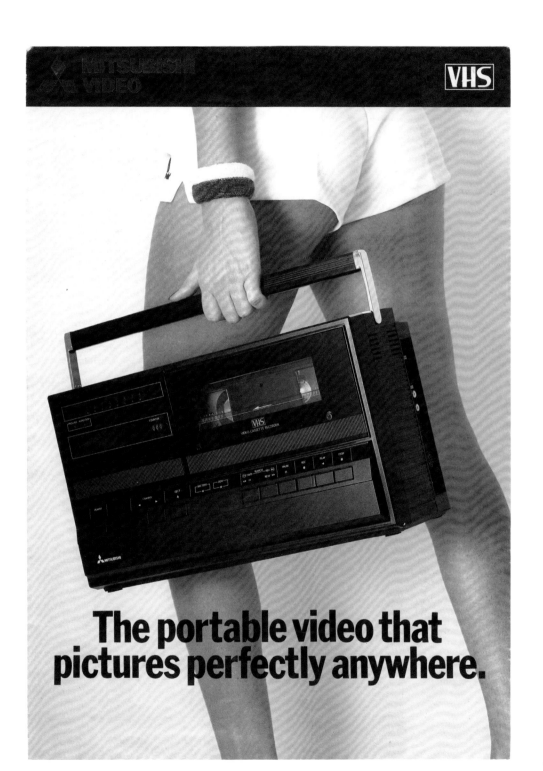

The portable video that pictures perfectly anywhere.

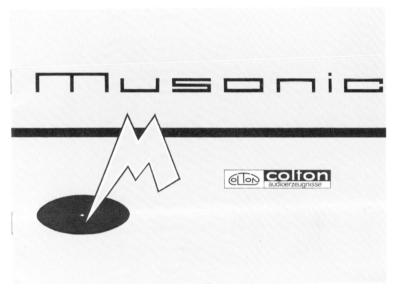

MUSONIC

This UK-based hi-fi stylus and accessories distribution company is still going strong after 70 years. And still uses the same logo.

MURPHY

Founded in 1929 and based in Welwyn Garden City, England. This radio manufacturer made sets for the British armed forces during World War II, most notably the Wireless Set No. 38, a battery-powered, portable valve apparatus, carried in a backpack. After the war, they produced several more models for naval use, while also starting to manufacture televisions. In 1962 the company was amalgamated into Bush Radio. Dating from the late 1960s, this very odd brochure shows a man looking at a woman who is staring at a TV that is switched off. Perhaps the scene makes sense if you consider their advertsing slogan: 'Murphy. Television that turns *you* on.' The brand still survives, but only as a licensed name in the Far East.

Murphy
vision

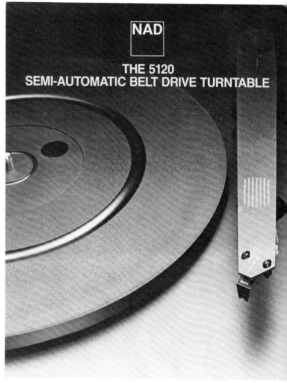

NAGRA

This Swiss company was set up in 1951 by Stefan Kudelski; the name translates as 'to record' in Polish. They are the de-facto sound-recording equipment for the movie industry and don't even bother trying your hand at field recordings unless you have a Nagra. These iconic objects have starred in a number of audio-centric Hollywood feature films, including *Klute* (1971), *The Conversation* (1974) and *Blow Out* (1981). Shown here is the classic SN (Série Noire) model, originally commissioned by President Kennedy and produced exclusively for the Central Intelligence Agency, before being made commercially available in the early 1970s. It even comes with a baby Nagra amplifier too. I mean 'wow'.

NAD

Standing for New Acoustic Dimension, this British company was founded in London in 1972 by electrical engineer, Dr Martin L. Borish. It was his ambition to 'cut through the hype' of the major audio brands by manufacturing hi-fi separates that represented excellent value for money, without compromising on sound or design. It certainly worked; NAD created great products with genuinely useful features, housed in cool, understated designs. My first proper deck was a NAD. Loved it.

NAGRA® SN

Magnétophone professionnel miniature

LABOACUSTICA s.r.l.
9, via L. Settembrini - Tel. 381955 - 355506
00195 ROMA

KUDELSKI S.A.

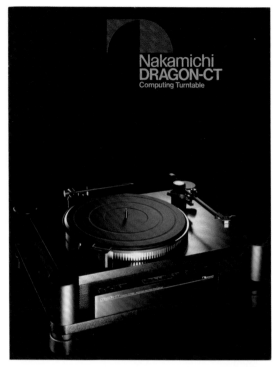

NAKAMICHI

Originally founded by Etsuro Nakamichi as the Nakamichi Research Corporation in 1948. Initially researching and developing audio and optics, the company quickly moved into manufacturing. After making tape machines for other companies (such as Fisher and Sansui) in 1973 they started making their own branded tech. They went on to produce groundbreaking tape machines and recorders, with almost fetishistic ideas and concepts, such as self-centring record players, flip-auto reverse and the world's first three-head cassette deck. All models are now highly desirable on the collectors' market. It's also worth noting that a sexy Nakamichi RX-505 and Dragon deck makes an appearance in the erotic romantic drama *9½ Weeks*.

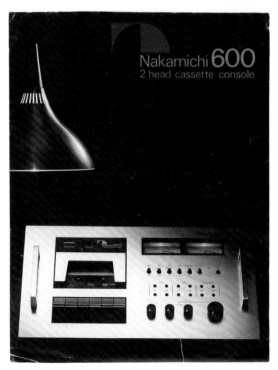

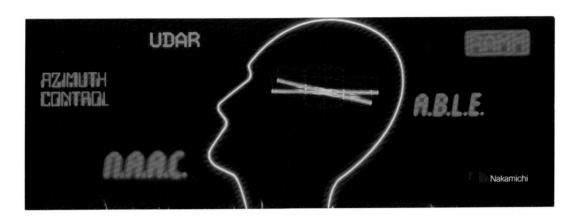

The Little Tape Recorder with the Big Sound.

NORELCO
101
TRANSISTOR
PORTABLE

NORELCO

I love Philips, for all sorts of reasons. They made great records, interesting products, lightbulbs, all sorts. Here they are again – Norelco is an acronym for **Nor**th American Philips [**el**ectrical] **Co**mpany that was set up in the 1940s to manufacture electrical products. They were prevented from using the 'Philips' name, as a court ruled that it was too similar to that of 'Philco' – potentially causing damage to the latter brand through consumer confusion and trademark infringement. Anyway, they made a range of products, from electric razors to tape machines. Philips eventually bought Philco in 1981, and were then allowed to use their own name, however, they also continued to use Norelco.

NATIONAL

National was a brand name used by Panasonic (see p136) to sell electronic products. The whole lot (National and Panasonic) was actually part of an empire built from humble beginnings by Konosuke Matsushita, when he started making electric lights for bicycles in the 1920s. He named the company 'National' in the hope that his products would be used across the whole of Japan. By 1988 National Panasonic was combined into a single brand.

NOVABEAM

This is Henry Kloss again (see Acoustic Research p12, and KLH p112). Here he is in 1982, inventing the Advent NovaBeam Projector for television. The first incarnation of this groundbreaking technology (the Advent VideoBeam 1000) was so darn good that it won Kloss an Emmy Award. Despite having to be projected onto a dedicated, slightly curved, screen (apparently off-centre viewing was poor) the science behind this apparatus is pretty advanced, involving such things as vacuum envelopes, which I do not understand at all.

NOVA

This very odd, but highly original, piece of failed equipment was put together by a company called Electronic Technological Innovations. I cannot find any information about the company or the colour wheel, but I really want one. I assume it changes depending on the music you play. Or maybe it's not that advanced.

NOVABEAM™
MODEL ONE
PROJECTION COLOR TELEVISION

If you are considering a large-screen projection color television set, the NOVABEAM Model One is well worth more than a casual look. It offers unprecedented overall performance, at a cost hundreds of dollars less than previous serious designs. Its combination of commanding picture size, high brightness, clarity, ease of operation, and elegantly simple engineering is unique. It has been designed to offer the serious television viewer the absolute maximum return on investment, a new standard of value in projection television for the home.

✳ SIMULATED TV PICTURE

watched any good music lately?

NOVA 30-2

PROGRAMMABLE 30" SQ.
NOVALITE COLOR WHEEL BY

NOVALITE COLOR WHEEL PLAYS MUSIC IN COLOR
8 programming switches provide countless pattern possibilities

ELECTRONIC TECHNOLOGICAL INNOVATIONS, INC.

ORTOFON

This Danish company are the world's largest manufacturer of phonograph cartridges, selling around 500,000 every year. Since 1918 they have been producing high-quality audio equipment. In 1945 they pioneered the use of moving coil technology in gramophone record cutting equipment. Elements of their early stylus designs and innovations can still be seen their fine contemporary products. The DJ market currently accounts for about three quarters of their stylus sales.

OPTIMUS RADIO

This Spanish audio giant was established in 1935. Initially starting with the manufacture of radios, the company moved into televisions in the 1960s. In the process, they developed some of the most bizarre brochure concepts I've ever come across. However, these must have worked, as the company still survives as a high-end commercial audio innovator.

ACCURACY IN SOUND
CARTRIDGES AND ACCESSORIES

OPTIMUS, S.A.
Gerona-España

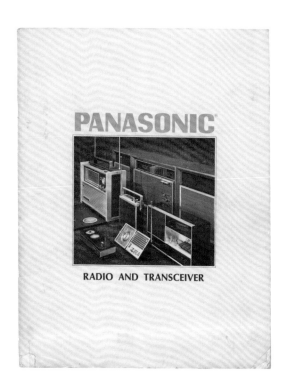

RADIO AND TRANSCEIVER

PANASONIC

Originally founded in 1918 by Konosuke Matsushita (known as the 'God of Mangement' in Japan) as a lightbulb socket manufacturer. Between 1935 and 2008 the company was known as Matsushita Electric Industrial Co. Ltd, then between 2008 and 2022 as the Panasonic Corporation, after which it became a holding company and was renamed as Panasonic Holdings Corporation. Originally its electronic products were marketed under the National brand (see p130), but in 1955 they began manufacturing export speakers with the name PanaSonic on them. This name was then adopted for the American market, as there was already a US company called National. This Japanese multinational conglomerate corporation, headquartered in Kadoma, Osaka, was the world's largest producer of consumer electronics in the late 20th century. Today Panasonic offers a bewildering range of products and services, including rechargeable batteries, automotive and avionic systems, industrial systems, as well as home renovation and construction – and don't forget that Technics (see p208) was just one of their many brands. Interesting to note that they fell into the 'Mondrian-style' marketing trap of the 1980s, along with everyone else.

Panasonic

TELEVISION ■ VIDEO ■ AUDIO ■ HOME AUTOMATION

The State of the Art

1989

RX-6600LE

RX-5300LE

TAPE RECORDERS

RX-5500LE □□ DOLBY SYSTEM

4-Band FM/LW/MW/SW Stereo Radio with Stereo Cassette Recorder and Dolby NR System

RX-5300LE
Portable 4-Band (FM/MW/LW/SW) Stereo Radio Cassette recorder with TPS

SG-1030L

SG-3000

MUSIC CENTRES

SG-1030L
Complete stereo Music Centre (Radio/Tape/Phono)

SG-3000
Complete Stereo Music Centre (Radio/Tape/Phono) □□ DOLBY SYSTEM

RF-504

RF-1103DLBE

RF-1110DLBE

RADIO

RF-504

RF-1105DLBE
4-Band (FM/LW/MW/SW) Portable Radio with LED Tuning Indicator, 1-IC and 5-Transistor

RF-1103DLBE
3-Band (FM/LW/MW) Portable Radio, 10-Transistor

RF-1110DLBE
4-band (FM/LW/MW/SW) Portable Radio, 1-IC, 1-FET and 15-Transistor

Panasonic

Video & TV
Music Centre
Hi-Fi
Radio
Tape Recorder
In-car Entertainment
Microwave Oven
Electronic Organ

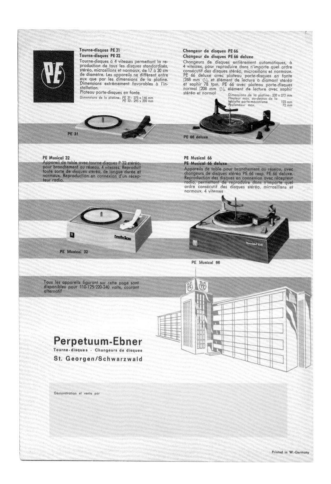

PERPETUUM-EBNER

I love this kind of industrial-style brochure. No flashy photography, no hip front room, no women lying down in front of anything. Instead Perpetuum-Ebner decided on a hard and straight style: here's our kit and here's the factory in the Black Forest where our high-end mechanical musical items have been produced since 1911. In 1951 they introduced their P-E Rex protable model, which went on to sell more than a million units over the next six years, making them the largest manufacturer of turntables in Europe. In 1971 the company merged with Dual (see p65) and in 1973, the Perpetuum-Ebner brand was no longer marketed. The company was relaunched as a fine turntable manufacturer in 2014.

ue perfectionnée

e extraordinaire
de reproduction

tes et modernes

leure idée

sique avec

62/63

m-Ebner

angeurs de disques

sound recording tape
bandes magnetiques
tonband
cinta magnetica
geluidsband

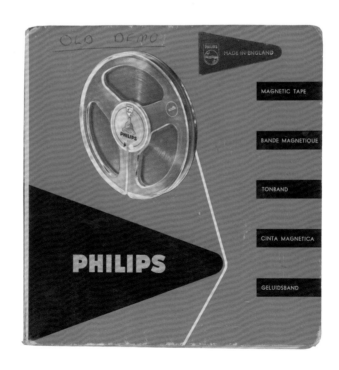

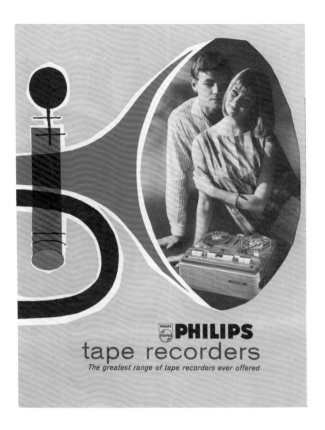

PHILIPS

This Dutch multinational conglomerate was founded in 1891 by Gerard Philips and his father Frederik. Originally producing lightbulbs, the company moved into electric shavers in 1939 with their Philishave, Norelco (see p130) and Ladyshave brands. In 1949 they began selling television sets and in 1950 established Philips Records which, with Siemens, formed part of PolyGram in 1962. After developing the compact cassette format in 1963, they were the first to produce a combined radio and cassette player (1966). Marketed as the 'radio recorder' they became commonly known as 'boomboxes'. In 1972 they launched the first consumer home video cassette recorder, the N1500, which used a bulky tape cassette. After persisting with a number of different models and improving tape duration, this system was eventually crushed by VHS and Betamax in the videotape format war (see Pye p154). In 1982, they developed the compact disc (alongside Sony, see p192), which in turn evolved into CD-R, DVD and Blu-ray (1997). Following a period of decline, the company restructured, retaining some of its electrical concerns, but also branching out into new areas such as healthcare.

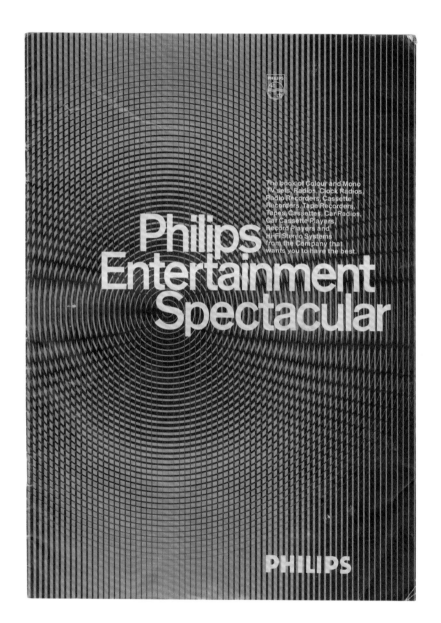

Philips
Entertainment
Spectacular

The book of Colour and Mono
TV sets, Radios, Clock Radios,
Radio Recorders, Cassette
Recorders, Tape Recorders,
Tapes, Cassettes, Car Radios,
Car Cassette Players,
Record Players and
Hi-Fi Stereo Systems
from the Company that
wants you to have the best.

PHILIPS

PHILIPS QUALITY
CASSETTES

Television

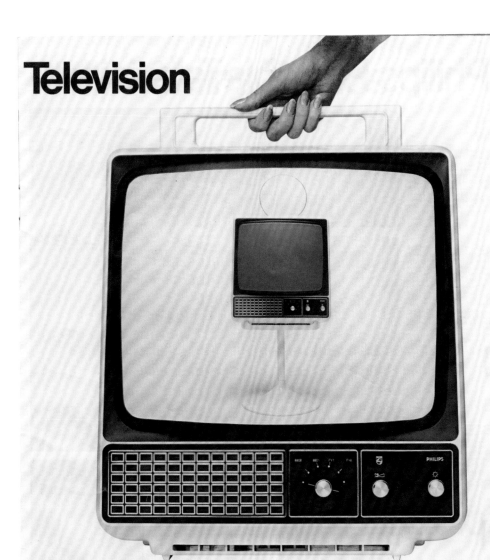

320
17" tube. The full-size TV that's portable. All-solid-state electronics include 4 integrated circuits, giving outstanding reliability, and saving so much space that the cabinet is only 12⅝" deep. Receives all programmes on 625-line UHF. The loop aerial provided is rotatable for optimum reception. Hinged carrying handle in recess on top of cabinet. Pedestal stand included.
Dimensions overall: 29½" high x 16⅝" wide x 12½" deep.

No need to break away from a good programme when you're preparing a meal or eating in a kitchen/dinette. Take the Philips 320 with you.

When somebody's ill it really is useful to have a TV you can easily carry into the bedroom – with a screen big enough to avoid strain.

Big enough for the lounge, light enough to carry around, elegant enough for anywhere. The Philips 320. The full-size TV that's portable.

Philips Audio 1984

PHILIPS

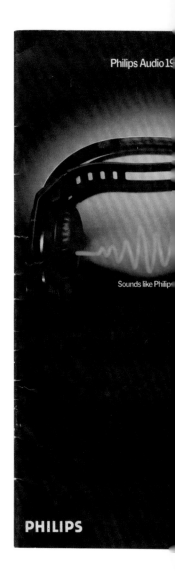

Philips Audio 19

Sounds like Philips

PHILIPS

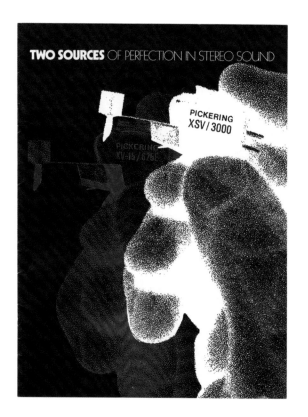

PIONEER

A Japanese manufacturer of all things electronic since 1938. Founded by Nozomu Matsumoto, the company started life as a humble Tokyo audio repair shop. As he was the son of a Christian missionary, the company was orignally named the Gospel Electric Company, reflecting his faith and belief that electronic products would help missionary work. In 1937 he invented the 'Pioneer' speaker and, after World War II, the company expanded rapidly, growing into a large multinational. They have many innovations under their belt, including the first removable car stereo, the first 'separate' stereo system, the first in-car compact disc player (1984), as well as playing a major role in the development of Blu-ray and LaserDisc technologies. I got quite obsessed by Pioneer (about the time I got hit by the motorbike), and used to try and draw the Pioneer logo quite a lot.

PICKERING

This American company was founded by Norman Pickering in 1945. Pickering, frustrated with the quality of sound from his phonograph records, took matters into his own hands, developing a pick up that reduced the wear on records while significantly increasing the fidelity of sound. In the dynamic field of cartridges and pick ups, Pickering holds more patents than any other company in the world. The company was bought by Stanton in 1950. Pickering went into ultrasound research, where he developed methods of detecting eye disease.

the
sound
of

PIONEER

CAR
STEREO

PIONEER

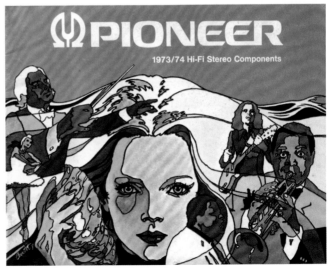

PIONEER

1973/74 Hi-Fi Stereo Components

TURNTABLES

"CAUTION: infringement of copyright and changes in specifications — see spec page"

PL-333
Fully Automatic Belt-Drive Turntable
- **Fully automatic operation:** To provide easy hands-off operation.
- **Low-mass straight tone arm:** Highly sensitive and resistant to resonance, tracks records better.
- **Precision DC servo motor:** Pioneer Stable Hanging Rotor ends spindle wobble for smoother and more accurate platter rotation.
- **Universal-type cartridge connector.**

PL-223
Auto-Return Belt-Drive Turntable
- **Low-mass straight tone arm:** Highly sensitive and resistant to resonance, tracks records better.
- **Auto-return convenience.**
- **Precision DC servo motor:** Pioneer Stable Hanging Rotor ends spindle wobble for smoother and more accurate platter rotation.
- **Universal-type cartridge connector.**

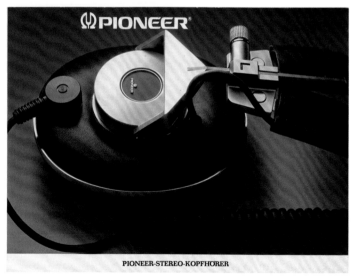

PIONEER-STEREO-KOPFHÖRER

152

Pyeaudio

WAKE UP TO WHAT PYE IS DOING

Portable audio
and in-car entertainment

PYE

This Cambridge-based company, founded by William Pye in 1896, began life maunfacturing scientific instruments for teaching and research. World War I increased demand and gave the company the technical knowlege to develop wireless radio receivers, as the first broadcasts were made by the BBC. They then developed television receivers (five-inch television sets) and eventually diversified into music, records, TV production and more (they even made the hand-held radios used by agents Bodie and Doyle in the UK television series *The Professionals*). The company has a rich history of innovations and disaster, getting into financial difficulty (largely thanks to cheaper Japanese competition) and somehow saving itself through chance or big sell offs. In 1979 the British investigative programme *World in Action* implicated the company in the supply of radios and telephone intercept equipment to Idi Amin's secret police in Uganda. The Pye Chelsea range of colour television sets, although unable to receive the imminent Channel 4 in the UK, were popular with rental companies such as Radio Rentals, Rumbelows and Wigfalls, who used them until the late 1980s. Pye was sold to Philips in 1976 who continued the brand and famously produced the V2000 video format along with Grundig (see the 20VR22 player brochure), which was also a disaster, eventually losing out to the cheaper and more popular VHS.

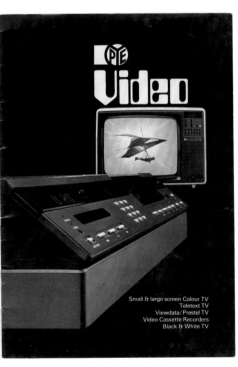

QUAD

QUAD Electroacoustics, a quintessential English company, was founded by Peter Walker in 1936. The name is an acronym for Quality Unit Amplifier Domestic, and was actually only adopted as the company name in 1983 after the launch of the QUAD I amplifier (their actual company name was the Acoustical Manufacturing Co. Ltd, even though everyone called them QUAD). Their first valve amplifiers were produced in 1948 and adopted by the BBC. They followed these with a series of consistently superb valve, and then transistor-powered models – all with a charming and timeless aesthetic appeal. Their Electrostatic Loudspeakers (ESL), introduced in 1957, have always been known for their transparency (a word that in the realm of audio means that sound is reproduced so perfectly, that you have no idea where the speakers are situated in the room). As with the amplifiers, the ESL speakers were also taken up by the BBC. In 1995 QUAD was bought by the Verity Group and is now part of the Chinese International Audio Group. Reassuringly, QUAD still service their original equipment if you send it to them.

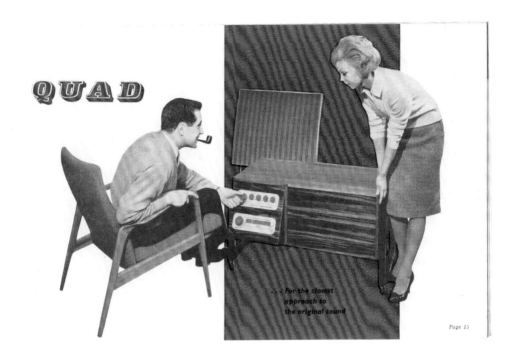

QUAD

... For the closest
approach to
the original sound

Page 15

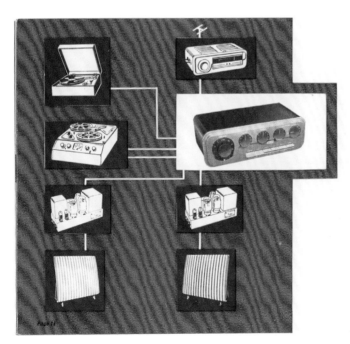

Page 11

VALVES

2 x EF86 (Z.729 or 6267),
2 x ECC83 (12AX7).

MECHANICAL

Front panel:	Die cast, stove finished silver fawn.
Knobs:	Matt brown.
Chassis:	Steel: Cadmium plated.
Cover:	Steel: Stoved steel grey.

The complete unit is electrically and mechanically suitable for use in all climatic conditions.

for the closest approach to the original sound......

QUAD

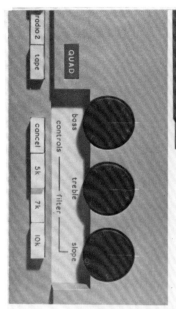

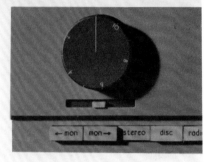

QUAD
for the closest approach to
the original sound

QUAD 33 CONTROL UNIT – QUAD 303 POWER AMPLIFIER
QUAD FM STEREO TUNER – QUAD ELECTROSTATIC LOUDSPEAKER

RCA Microphones Select-A-Guide

RCA VICTOR PRESENTS THE
WORLD'S GREATEST ARTISTS
ON 4-TRACK 7½ I.P.S.
LIVING STEREO REEL TAPES

RCA

The Radio Corporation of America was founded in 1919 – a titan across the fields of electrical goods manufacturing, audio recordings and cinema, as well as being a pioneer of television. Among all this, they still found the time to make some impressive industry-standard equipment and got involved in every new format that came along. Today the company exists as a brand name only, while its various trademarks are now used by a number of multinationals.

REGA RESEARCH

This British audio manufacturing and engineering company was established in 1973. The name is derived from the surnames of the two founders – Tony **RE**lph and Roy **GA**ndy. In 1977 they introduced the revolutionary Rega Planar 3 – an affordable, functional and aesthetically pleasing turntable that formed the bedrock of the company for the next 30 years. Today this excellent and innovative company has 150 employees, hand assembles its product and has no marketing department.

RCF (RADIO CINE FORNITURE)

Based in Reggio Emilia, this Italian audio company was established in 1949. They originally sold microphones. In the 1960s, as music performances became increasingly electric rather than acoustic, they jumped on the concert tour bus and started getting heavily involved with live music technology. Today the RCF Arena (in their home town) is Europe's largest permanent outdoor events space.

REVOX

Will Studer, a Swiss entrepreneur founded ReVox in 1948 to make tape recorders. He used the ReVox name on machines aimed at the amateur consumer market, while the Studer name was used on high-end equipment manufactured for professionals. From 1950 onwards the company produced some of the greatest reel to reel recorders (pretty much industry standard), speakers and even linear tracking record players.

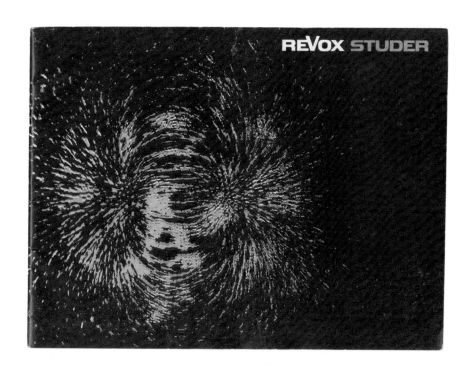

B215

Cassette Tape Recorder

easyline

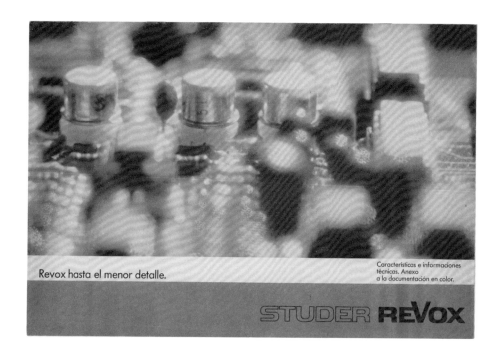

Revox hasta el menor detalle.

Características e informaciones técnicas. Anexo a la documentación en color.

STUDER REVOX

High Fidelity
Reflex Enclosures *by* Richard Allan

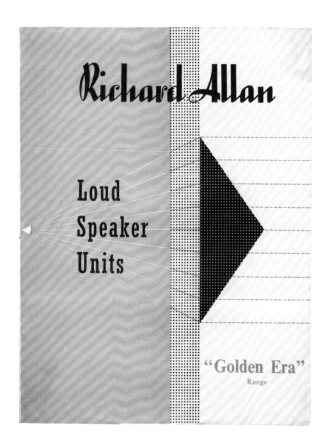

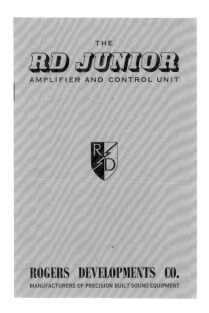

RICHARD ALLAN

The origins of this company go back to 1949, when Richard Allan Radio was started. The name comes from the two founders' sons (yes, that's right: Richard and Allan). Based in Batley, Yorkshire, they manufactured very fine speakers by reverse engineering the market-leading product of the time and making a slightly more affordable version.

RD JUNIOR CORNER HORN
(Fitted louvred side panels)

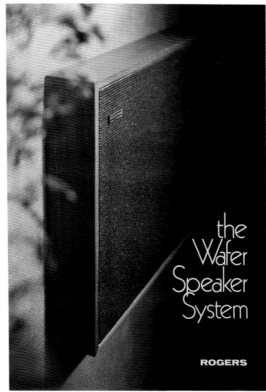

ROGERS

Based in Hampstead, North London, this company started life as Rogers Developments in 1947, introducing the RD Junior Speaker and amplifier in 1948. Consistently making and improving their high-end speaker and amplifier systems, in 1972 the company was approved under licence to manufacture BBC-designed speakers – top-drawer stuff. In 1975 Rogers obtained a further licence from the BBC to manufacture the legendary LS3/5A – a small, natural-sounding studio monitor. In the same year, Jim Rogers, the founder, left to start a new venture and the company went bankrupt. It was subsequently bought by Swisstone, a trading company owned jointly by the former chairman and managing director of Rogers. The company, now reborn and rebadged, began to thrive once more and in 1993 it was sold to Wo Kee Holdings. In 1998, Rogers finally ceased manufacturing in the UK.

SABA

The origins of the Schwarzwälder Apparate-Bau-Anstalt company date back to 1835 when it was making cuckoo clocks in the Black Forest, becoming a radio manufacturer in 1927, producing over 100,000 units annually by 1931. SABA entered the burgeoning broadcasting business in 1951 with the production of their first television. The company continued to expand into numerous consumer electronics sectors, simultaneously producing innovative new products, such as wireless television remotes. In 1975 it was bought by the American company GT International, then in 1980 sold on to European consumer electronics brand Thomson-Brandt. 1994 sees a groovy collab with Philippe Starck, producing a range of kooky products such as 'Boa', speakers that look a bit like a scarf or a bra (depending on how you wear them), and 'Street Master', a speaker that resembles a spear. The company still thrives today. Forgot to mention they also started a record subsidiary in the 1960s, dropping some solid modern jazz.

SABA

TV·Video·HiFi
1983/84

The
Bright
One

Model 7619
19″ diagonal 100% solid state deluxe color TV with remote control

SAMPO

This electronics firm was established in 1936, making household electronics from washing machines to televisions and everything in between. They joined forces with Sony in 1967 to form Sony Taiwan Limited, a partnership which ended in 2000. The firm was listed on the Taiwan Stock Exchange in 1970 and by 1979 was a top ten company. In 1996 one of the owners, Chen Maobang, helped establish the Taiwan Baseball League, which was merged with the Chinese Baseball League in 2003. Let's hope their graphic style has improved since the mid-1970s.

SANYO

This electronics-based firm was established in Osaka, in 1949. The name translates as 'three oceans', signifying a desire to sell their products across the Pacific, Atlantic and Indian Oceans, and consequently, the world. The company had produced Japan's first plastic radio by 1952. They expanded rapidly, bringing in Howard Ladd, a new and daring American executive vice president, in 1969. Ladd introduced Sanyo to the USA, handling the purchase of Fisher in 1975 (see p80). Under his guidance Sanyo invested heavily in television advertising, a strategy which paid off, the firm becoming a multi-million-dollar industry leader. After successfully focussing on lithium batteries and developing the first hybrid solar cell in 1992, the company suffered financial difficulties following huge over investment in semiconductors. In 2009 it was bought by Panasonic (see p136) and the brand was completely discontinued in 2011.

SANYO

Catalogo Generale

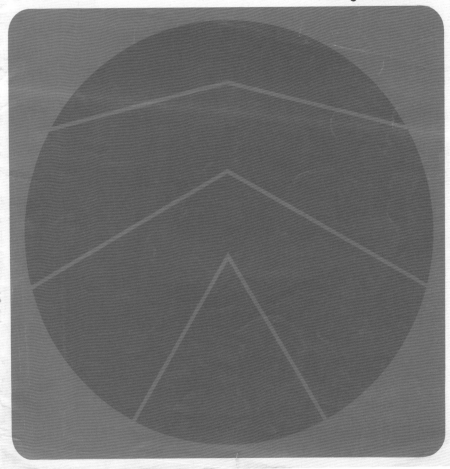

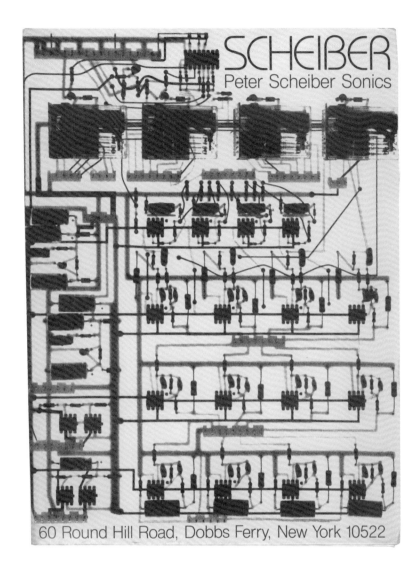

SCHEIBER
Peter Scheiber Sonics

60 Round Hill Road, Dobbs Ferry, New York 10522

PETER SCHEIBER SONICS

American Peter Scheiber was a gifted musician and technical wizard – a somewhat lethal combination. As a young man he'd play his bassoon as first chair (leader of that instrument section) in many orchestras, while also tinkering with electronics trying to make music sound more lifelike. In 1968 he developed an encoder and decoder system that created 'surround sound' from multiple speakers. After patenting this technology, he demonstrated his new quadraphonic system to various record companies, including CBS and Ray Dolby. He agreed a licensing deal with CBS; however, other labels simply copied the technology, engineering their own inferior quad versions. He devised his own 360º Spatial Decoder (sold at high-end industry fairs) and later attempted to sue Dolby for infringements of his various 'surround sound' patents which, through its use in both cinemas and homes, had made that company millions. Scheiber managed to get limited royalties, but the battle took a toll; he sadly spent eight years as a recluse, while Dolby claimed his patents and rights had expired. He countersued and lost, and spent the rest of his life trying to invent something else.

SANSUI

Kosaku Kikuchi started Sansui in 1947 to manufacture radio parts because he thought their quality could be improved. He began making amplifier kits and produced a series of very fine audio amplifiers throughout the 1960s. In 1971, Sansui introduced the Quadphonic Synthesizer QS-1, that created four-channel stereo from two-channel sources. Their amplifiers grew in popularity, stature and reputation, but huge competition from other Japanese companies narrowed their market share. The company ceased trading in 2014. And finally, I have to mention the penthouse flat featured in this brochure. It looks just like the one from *Theatre of Blood*, where Vincent Price chucks himself off the balcony.

SCHNEIDER

This German company started life in 1889, manufacturing
woodworking tools. In the 1960s they entered the hi-fi
market via cabinet making, creating a series of low-cost
entry-level hi-fi systems for the not too discerning punter.
In the 1980s they got into the all new personal computer
market, before eventually going bankrupt in 2002.

SCHNEIDER HI-FI

1971-72

Length	1⅞ ips	3¾ ips	7½ ips	15 ips
200 ft playing time	42m	21m	10m	5m

Dual-track times

Scotch recording tapes

playing time **CALCULATOR**

Price 6d.

SCOTCH

This famous American tape brand has origins going back to the Depression era. In 1925, a 3M engineer by the name of Richard Drew invented masking tape, and followed this in 1935 with a clear sticky tape that became popular with households who needed to make do and mend in hard times. The brand name came about after a less than positive reaction from an engineer who was testing the product; he remarked 'take this tape back to those Scotch bosses of yours and tell them to put more adhesive on it!' 'Scotch' being a derogatory term meaning 'frugal'. The Scotch name stuck – and the company went on to expand into all areas of tape, including the burgeoning audio sector in the 1950s. Scotty McTape, a cartoon boy wearing a kilt, was the brand mascot from the mid-1940s and the company still uses tartan in their branding today.

THE HOW TO DO IT booklet of tape recording

Trade Mark
Scotch
magnetic tape

3M

2400 FT | 730 M

D 7 ins | 18 cm P

200

POLYESTER

Scotch **Professional Recording Tape**

3M

FOUR TRACK

A NEW DIMENSION IN TAPE RECORDING

the Scottie

**AM/FM/FM/ STEREO
MUSIC SYSTEM**
An entirely new concept
in listening enjoyment
ONLY $199.95 — COMPLETE!

SCOTT STEREO '70

2501

SCOTT STEREO PHONOGRAPH

SCOTT

This compact
phono system gives you
Scott component features
plus built-in Scott performance and reliability, at
modest cost. Dual Bass, Treble, and Volume controls let you
adjust each channel to suit your tastes and room acoustics.
Mic/guitar input, connections for tape recorder, extra speakers,
separate tuner, and stereo headphones give you a range of
musical enjoyment that you just won't find in any other stereo
system at this price.

2504

SCOTT FM STEREO PHONOGRAPH

FM, FM stereo, and your favorite records take on a new dimension
of reality, when heard on Scott's agreeably-priced 2504. You
enjoy superb Scott component performance on FM and FM stereo
plus a professional automatic turntable, with magnetic
cartridge and diamond stylus. Scott's patented automatic stereo
switching knows when a stereo program is being broadcast,
and automatically turns itself to stereo operation.

Great Scott compact stereo music systems

H. H. SCOTT INC. 111 POWDERMILL RD MAYNARD MASSACHUSETTS

SCOTT

Hermon Hosmer Scott established his audio company in 1947. Based in Massachusetts, they were at the forefront of amplification technology throughout the 1950s and produced some superb equipment, both for the home and scientific markets. The company ceased trading in 1972 as funds to expand ran dry.

SEAS
PROFESSIONAL
SOUND

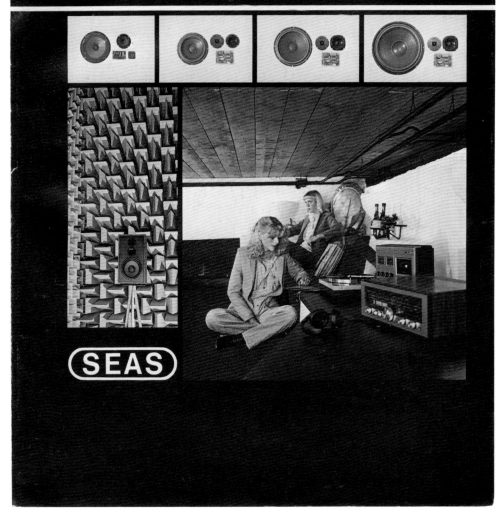

SEAS

DD TOWER

The DD-Tower is a 4-way loudspeaker system, consisting of two cabinets, a top cabinet and a sub-woofer cabinet. The sub-woofer cabinet is of the bass reflex type, with the port at the bottom of the cabinet. The SEAS DD-Tower uses the sub-woofer principle in its most optimal way, by making it an integrated part of the system. The sub-woofer crosses over at approximately 180 Hz, thereby sharing the most powerful part of the frequency range with the woofer in the top-cabinet. The top-cabinet is a 3-way system with the woofer in a dual chamber. This ensures good transient reproduction and eliminates the problems at the crossover frequency when crossing in the sub-woofer-system. The drive units are placed in line on the front-baffle.The angle of the sloped front and the distance between the units are calculated very closely in order to give a correct time response at

The DD-Tower has separate regulators for the tweeter and mid-range units. The level can be raised and lowered 1.5 dB and in this way be adjusted to the interior in the listening room. The drive unit in the sub-woofer is fitted with Dynamic Damping (DD). This is a recently developed and patented system, which eliminates the problems with transient distortion at high power levels in bass reflex systems.
The «boominess» often connected with bass reflex systems, and which is caused by the large delayed cone excursions, is therefore not present.
The Dynamic Damping system acts as an electromagnetic

listening position. This means that the acoustical centres of the units are placed on a vertical line so that the sound contribution from each unit reaches the listeners ear simultaneously.
The cabinet front is covered with acoustic transparent black foam. This material is chosen because of its very good transparency at all frequencies. This also eliminates the problems of sound reflections from a clothframe.

shock absorber preventing the oscillations caused by the delayed excursions at high power levels.

Frequency range: 28-25000 Hz — Crossover frequency: 180 Hz, 600 Hz, 4000 Hz
Nominal power: 120 W — Music power: 200 W — Characteristic sensitivity: 90 dB
Operating power: 4 W — Impedance: 8 ohm — Recommended amplifier power: 30 W -200 W
Volume top cabinet: 25 litres — Volume sub-woofer cabinet: 60 litres
Total height: 1195 mm — Max. width: 451 mm
Max. depth: 350 mm — Weight: 32 kg

DISCO TOWER

The DISCO TOWER is designed to reproduce really high sound-pressure. The power handling capacity is 160 W (music power) and the sensitivity is 100 dB at 1 m with power input of 1 W.
The «mixture» of 2 woofers, 2 mid-ranges and 3 tweeters, one a horn-loaded tweeter all in a ported cabinet, gives an agressive and open sound in the mid-tweeter area, and a tremendous attack in the bass area.
Marvellous DISCO-SOUND!

On the front panel are mounted separate level controls for the midrange and tweeter units. The sound level can be raised and lowered 1.5 dB in order to achieve an optimal adjustment to the listening room. On the same panel are also mounted indicator lights for the automatic midrange/tweeter protection circuit. At extremely high power inputs the protection circuit will be activated and the lamps will light up. Disco Tower is supplied in black lacquered ash. The frame is covered with black strech-cloth.

Frequency range: 40-20.000 Hz. Crossover frequency: 900Hz, 2500 Hz, 6000 Hz
Nominal power: 120W. Music power: 160W. Characteristic sensitivity: 100 dB.
Operating power: 0.4W. Impedance: 8 ohm. Recomm. amplifier power: 6W - 160W.
Volume: 100 litres. Total height: 1250 mm. Max width: 580 mm.
Max. depth: 348 mm. Weight: 37 kg.

SEAS

In 1950 Norwegian radio manufacturers Radionette and Tandberg created Scandinavian Electro Acoustic Systems, a spinoff company with the aim of developing superior-quality loudspeakers. They succeeded in creating a long series of fine and desirable models, while broadening its range to include audio components for televisions. In 1977 SEAS patented 'DD-rings' as part of the Dynamic Damping concept (as featured in the brochure above). The company is very much alive and still at the progressive edge of sound and speaker technology. And yes, I really REALLY want a Disco Tower. I think we all do.

SENNHEISER

Started by Fritz Sennheiser in Germany just after World War II, the company was initially a laboratory researching microphone technology and manufacturing voltmeters. Within a few years the company had over 200 employees and was successfully producing quality microphones, transformers and magnetic headphones. Their equipment was often used by spies throughout the Cold War – in particular, the MM series of tiny microphones could easily be disguised to avoid detection. In 1980, Sennheiser were commissioned to supply in-flight headphones for Lufthansa passengers, and the classic Sennheiser HD-25 model, designed in 1988, was given to all Concorde passengers from 1989 onwards. Supersonic!

SHARP

Founded by Tokuji Hayakawa in 1912, the company name originates from his invention of the Ever-Ready 'Sharp' mechanical pencil in 1915, an international success. The company was devastated by the 1923 Kanto earthquake that hit Tokyo, but after relocating to Osaka, in 1925, they started producing some of the earliest Japanese radios. Over the following decades they successfully surfed various technological waves – television, calculators (for which they produced the first liquid-crystal display), hi-fi, domestic microwaves, computer games and the world's first camera phone. The company still operates on a global scale and is currently owned by Foxxcon. However, I do question the connection between boomboxes and steam trains.

QT-S360E

Fashionable Stereo Radio
Cassette with All Round
Speaker Design

•

All round sound system with
built-in computer analysed
diffuser

•

Durable shoulder strap for
listeners on-the-go

QT-F10E

Personal Cassette player
with two band radio. Shaped
in passionate red, green,
yellow, white or blue

•

Two-way carrying strap

•

Cassette with automatic stop
mechanism

•

FM/AM two band radio

•

Built-in microphone

𝓗OME ENTERTAINMENT
Collection '88

*portable
▸ audio ◂
COLLECTION
1988*

CA70

SHURE

This American company was established by Sidney Shure in Chicago, in 1925, selling radio kits from their mail order catalogue. After quick initial expansion, the advent of the Great Depression combined with the increased availability of factory-built radios saw the company shrink dramatically and move into the distribution of microphones. By 1931 they were manufacturing their own models, securing their first patent with the innovative microphone suspension support system. Within a few years had made some of the most important microphones of all time – the Model 55

Unidyne is perhaps one of the most recognisable ever made (Martin Luther King Jr. is talking into one for his 'I Have A Dream' speech; it was also frequently used by Elvis Presley). In the mid-1940s they began making phonograph cartridges, quickly becoming the country's largest producer. Shure was at the forefront of cartridge innovation (they were the first to use a 15° tilt for optimum tracking), and at their peak manufactured nearly 30,000 cartridges a day. This award-winning company still innovates and is still in private hands.

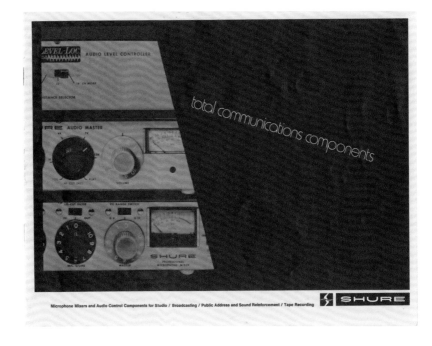

SIEMENS

Hi-Fi-Stereophonie bedeutet naturgetreues, unverfälschtes Hören von Stereo-Rundfunksendungen, Stereo-Schallplatten und Stereo-Tonbändern. Hi-Fi-Stereophonie — das ist Musik, wie Sie Musik lieben, Musik wie im Konzertsaal. Erleben auch Sie Stereophonie in Hi-Fi-Qualität mit der neuen Siemens-Stereo-Anlage

KLANGMEISTER 80

SIEMENS

Another vast conglomerate. This one was established in 1847 in Berlin, when Werner von Siemens and his business partner invented a successful telegraph machine that pointed at letters instead of beeping. In the 1920s and 1930s they were making microphones, radios and even electron microscopes. The company used forced labour during World War II and subsequently, at the end of the war, lost of 80 percent of its total worth along with all of its assets in reparation. Today the company works across a myriad of technologies and services, from healthcare to finance and digital industries.

SME

The name stands for Scale Model Equipment and the company was established in 1946 to manufacture scale models and parts for the engineering trade. In 1959 company founder Alastair Robertson-Aikman needed a new pick-up arm for his turntable, so got his own firm to make one. The result was enthusiastically received by his friends in the audio industry and so the first SME tonearms went into production. Their 9" and 12" arms were the broadcast standard throughout the 1960s and 1970s. Today the company makes high-end tonearms and unbelievably good turntables.

SME SERIES II

PRECISION PICK-UP ARMS models 3009 and 3012

The best *pick-up arm in the world*

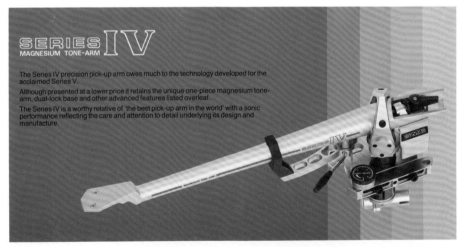

SERIES IV
MAGNESIUM TONE-ARM

The Series IV precision pick-up arm owes much to the technology developed for the acclaimed Series V.

Although presented at a lower price it retains the unique one-piece magnesium tone-arm, dual-lock base and other advanced features listed overleaf.

The Series IV is a worthy relative of 'the best pick-up arm in the world' with a sonic performance reflecting the care and attention to detail underlying its design and manufacture.

SME

The best pick-up arm in the world

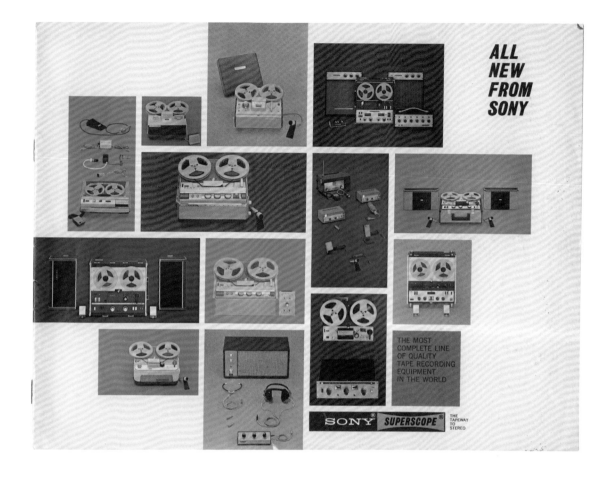

ALL NEW FROM SONY

THE MOST COMPLETE LINE OF QUALITY TAPE RECORDING EQUIPMENT IN THE WORLD

SONY® SUPERSCOPE® THE TAPEWAY TO STEREO

SONY

Who knew that a little Tokyo electronics shop would go on to become one of the world's largest electronics and technology companies? Opened in 1946 by Masaru Ibuka, the business grew fast. He was joined by Akio Morita a few months later and together they started the Tokyo Telecommunications Engineering Corporation, building the country's first tape recorder (AKA the talking paper machine) in 1950. They rebranded themselves SONY, a name chosen for it's likeness to 'sonny boy', a popular American term, and 'sonus', latin for 'sound'. With their new global name in place Sony expanded quickly, their 1957 miniature TR-63 radio opening the doors to the US marketplace, heralding a new era of exciting portable audio products. 1968 saw the introduction of Sony's patented

Trinitron technology, which turned Sony into the world's biggest manufacturer of televisions. Also in 1968 they introduced the TC-50 compact cassette recorder / player – a precursor to the Walkman – these machines were assigned to all NASA astronauts from Apollo 7 onwards, to record mission logs (although they took personal mixtapes into space, which were then recorded over). In 1975 they launched the Betamax video format (ultimately, unsuccessful), then in 1979 the Walkman (very successful, going on to sell in excess of 200 million units). In 1981 Sony produced the first compact disc (in collaboration with Philips, see p142) and the first compact disc player. They keep going. Dispite a few peaks and troughs, Sony remains a global force in innovation and technology.

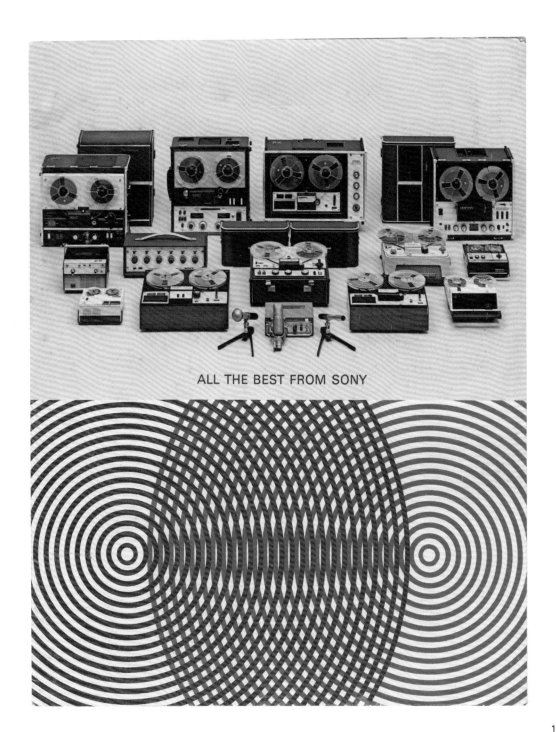

ALL THE BEST FROM SONY

VISIONS OF '74

ALL THE BEST FROM SONY!

Color Black White

salesmen's guide to SONY TV

SONY® RECORDING EQUIPMENT

あなたのオーディオ・ライフに新世界を切り開くソニー・生録音機器

COLOR TV
BLACK & WHITE TV
PROJECTION TV
BETAMAX
RADIO
TAPE RECORDERS
INTERLOCK SOUND SYSTEMS
SIMPLEX SOUND SYSTEMS

SONY

TPB-800
8-Track Cartridge Player

The sound of music is yours wherever you go . . . with the TPB-800.

For those who enjoy convenient music with pre-recorded 8-track cartridges — there's the TPB-800. Just slip in a tape, adjust tone and volume controls, and relax. Program selection is automatic — or manual, by simply pressing the program selector. Your choice of AC, DC or car-boat battery operation and a fold-down carrying handle make the TPB-800 completely portable. And ideal for any member of the family — at home or on-the-go

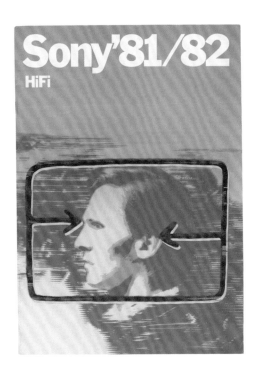

Sony'81/82

HiFi

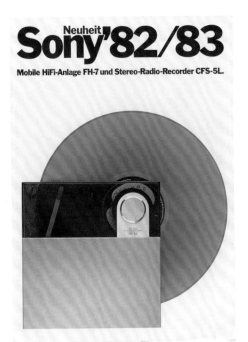

Neuheit
Sony'82/83

Mobile HiFi-Anlage FH-7 und Stereo-Radio-Recorder CFS-5L.

SONY

FM/AMラジオカセット
pro 1150
CF-1150 ¥39,800

肩にぶらぶらいい音録ったりいい音聞いたり

昭和50年4月現在の製品が掲載されています

SONY

ポケッタブルラジオ

総合カタログ

"ポータブル & ポケッタブル"、ソニーのワイド バラエティ。
個性あるラジオを個性的に使ってみてください。

Neuheit

Sony'83

Der Walkman®stellt seine Familie vor.

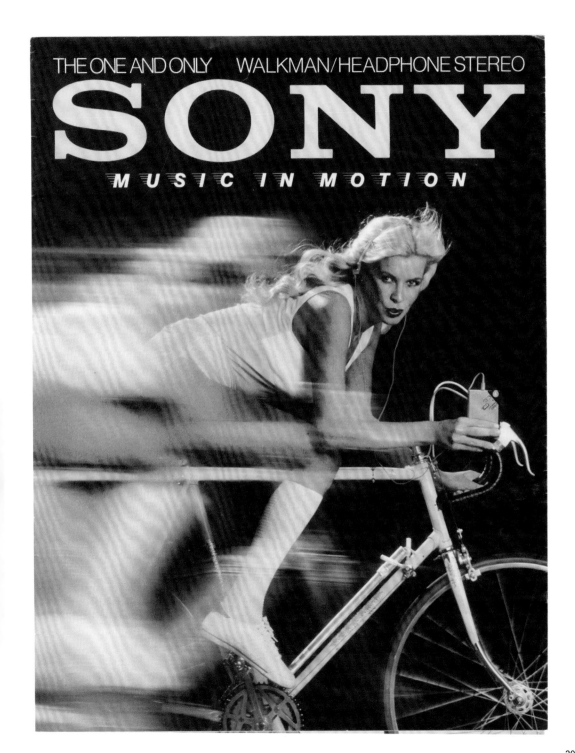

STRATHEARN

Welcome to the DeLorean of the hi-fi world. A government quango was set up in 1973 with the objective of stimulating economic growth in Northern Ireland. They decided to establish a government-funded hi-fi company, and, after several rounds of expensive and clueless research, settled on a plan to manufacture a turntable with fashionable direct-drive motor. However, the motors used in the prototype were taken from children's toys and were not powerful or precise enough to drive a turntable without sonic consequences. Manufacturing faults and launch disasters followed, and the company folded in 1979 owing millions, all thanks to a bunch of government clowns who had no idea what they were really doing. Sounds familiar.

SOUTHWEST TECHNICAL PRODUCTS CORPORATION

Daniel Meyer was a talented electronics engineer who designed and published projects for hobbyist electronics magazines in the early 1960s. In 1967 he spotted an opportunity, setting up STPC to sell the circuit boards and parts used in his newly published projects. The operation proved very popular and he began selling parts for projects published by other electrical engineers, ranging from hi-fi systems and amplifiers to metal detectors. Within seven years the company was shipping 100 kits a day. By the mid-1970s they'd moved into the microcomputer market, but as this area rapidly developed they found it harder to compete and in 1987 they focussed on point-of-sale computer systems, before ceasing to trade in 1990.

SOUTHWEST TECHNICAL PRODUCTS CORPORATION

TANDBERG

A Norwegian company founded by Vebjørn Tandberg in 1933 as an Oslo radio factory, making quality speakers and radiograms. In the early 1950s they moved into the reel to reel tape recorder market, pushing the technology and introducing new and innovative features over the next decade, including stereo playback, stereo recording and cross-field recordings. In a tragic turn of events, in 1978, following a major economic downturn, Vebjørn Tandberg was removed by shareholders and committed suicide. Subsequently, the company was declared bankrupt. The brand was later revived, only to be swallowed up by Cisco Systems in 2010.

TANNOY

The name Tannoy is an abbreviation of tantalum alloy, which is the primary element used in the electrolytic rectifier the company invented (this device sits inside pretty much all electric equipment and changes AC current to DC current). The company was started in London by Guy Fountain in 1926. Tannoy has became a generic term, thanks to their supplying superb (and prominently branded) speakers and public address systems to the military, Butlin's, Pontins and anyone else who wanted one. Their period home audio speakers and studio monitors (such as Tannoy Golds) are well engineered and hard to beat. The company is currently owned by The Music Tribe group of companies, based in the Philippines.

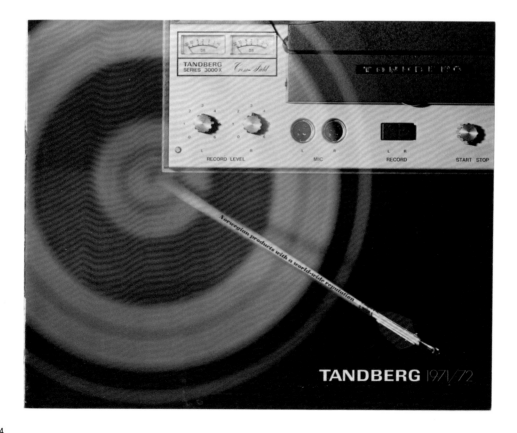

THE
TANNOY
G.R.F.
ENCLOSURE

TDK

My cassette tape of choice in the 1980s. TDK was founded in 1935 to manufacture the magnetic material ferrite. They began producing magnetic tapes in the 1950s, followed by compact cassettes in the 1960s, eventually manufacturing a huge range of recordable media, for numerous formats. In 1997, the company began to gradually withdraw from the production of compact cassettes. Since 2005, TDK has bought a large number of companies manufacturing and selling electronic components (such as power supplies for mobile phones).

TEAC

Teac is what happened when the Tokyo Television Acoustic Company and the Tokyo Electro-Acoustic Company merged in 1956. Basically they all worked out they could make better reel to reel machines than anyone else – so they did. In 1969 they produced the first quadraphonic reel to reel for the domestic consumer. Then in 1972 they developed the first affordable reel to reel technology for overdubbing, essentially allowing musicians to create the first home studios. Gibson bought the company in 2013. Then Gibson went bankrupt in 2018 and so TEAC declared they would continue operations on on their own.

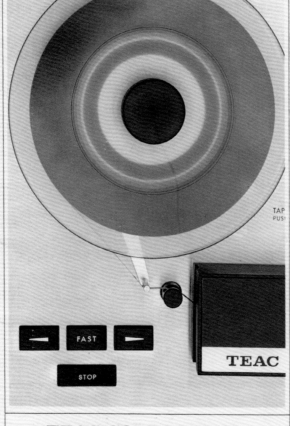

TEAC

AUDIO EQUIPMENT

TEAC CORPORATION

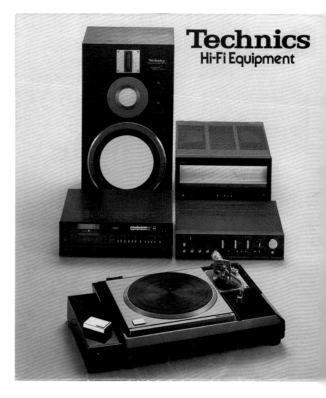

TECHNICS

Technics is the brand name used by Panasonic (see p136) for their audio products. From 1965, Technics manufactured products including turntables, ampilfiers, radios, etc., but things really started cooking with the introduction of the direct-drive turntable. In 1969, the SP-10 was the first commercial model (there's one on the front of the right-hand brochure above). I'd love one, however they are now very expensive. This was followed by the SL-1100 in 1971, which was soon adopted by DJs (Kool Herc used two for his 'merry-go-round' method of playing records) for what we now refer to as 'turntablism' – the direct-drive deck allowed the DJ to spin back records on them without inflicting any damage to the equipment, enabling the creation of new music and beats. This was followed in 1972 by the release of the SL-1200 – probably the most famous DJ deck in the world. These were manufactured until 2010; quite why they stopped making them is a mystery to me, but they still produce a derivative version. Anyway, the company are still going strong and have produced some classic audio products over the decades.

Technics

'84/'85

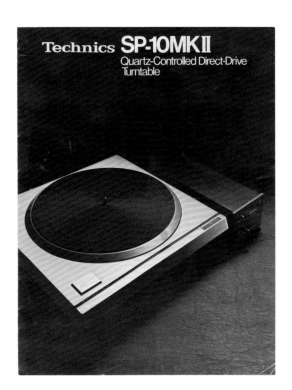

Technics SP-10MKII
Quartz-Controlled Direct-Drive
Turntable

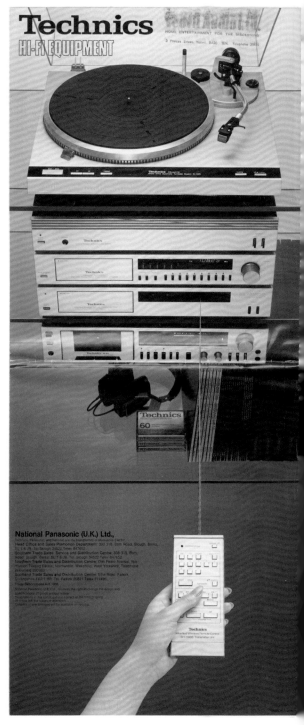

National Panasonic (U.K.) Ltd.,

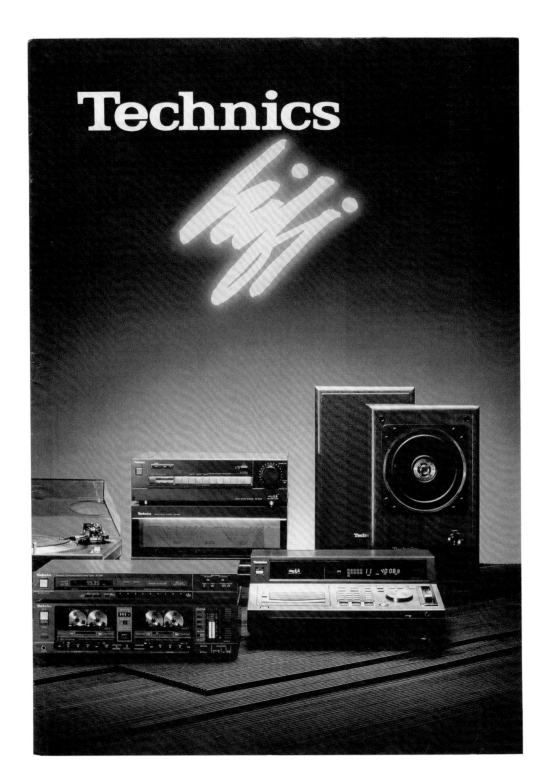

BROWN TO BLONDIE.

WORK WITH WAYLON.

SKATE TO STREISAND

IBM TO ELO.

TECHNIDYNE

Following on from the instant and phenomenal success of the Sony Walkman (1979/1980), several companies, including Technidyne, decided to produce similar technology. Like the Walkman, this personal stereo also included a 'hotline' button, whereby users could lower the volume of the audio to have a conversation without removing their headphones. This feature was added at the insistence of Sony chairman Akio Morita, who feared the technology would isolate the user. The button was removed from later models.

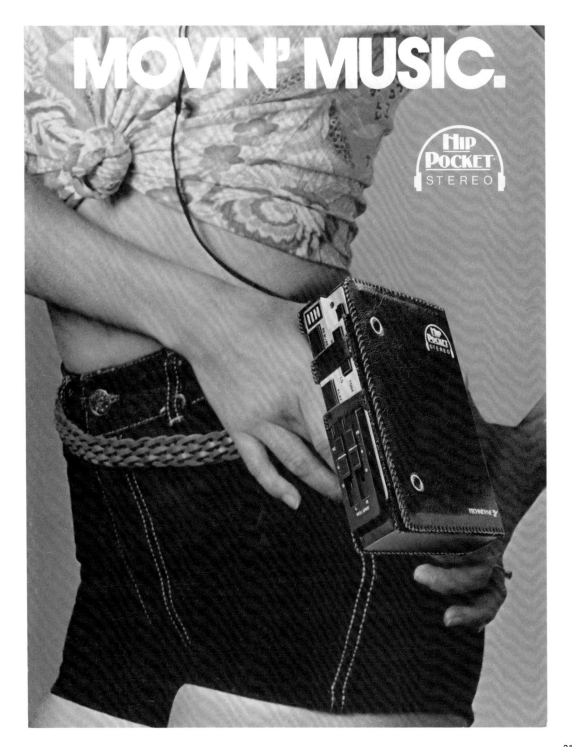

magnetophon 300

A tape recorder...
genuine portable
really versatile

TELEFUNKEN

TELEFUNKEN

This German joint venture between AEG and Siemens was started in 1903, after a dispute over patents between the two companies led to the intervention of Kaiser Wilhelm II, who persuaded them to join forces. Telefunken were major players in the rapidly growing communications business, thanks to their strong connections with the German military; they even devised radio navigation systems for Zeppelin airships. After World War I, they moved into broadcasting technology, producing radios from 1923 and the first commercial televisions in 1934. In 1936 they developed the first electronic television camera, which was used to broadcast live from the Berlin Olympics. Over the course of its history, Telefunken has made many notable innovations, from portable mobile radios to radar traffic control systems and lingual computers. The company has been bought and sold several times and still produces a range of products sold internationally. The original logo and name have been licensed by American Toni Roger Fishman, who restores old Telefunken technology and makes fine reproductions of vintage microphones.

THORENS

This Swiss company dates from 1883 and originally made musical boxes and clock movements, before beginning to manufacture phonographs in 1903. They produced their first electric record players in 1928, and by the 1950s were making superbly engineered platters that are still very much in demand with audiophiles today. The company suffered insolvency in 1999, but a new company rose from the ashes and still makes fine turntables today. Incidentally, Thorens also made amazing mechanical 'single claw' cigarette lighters from the 1920s onwards. I know because I had one back in the day, when I used to smoke roll-ups.

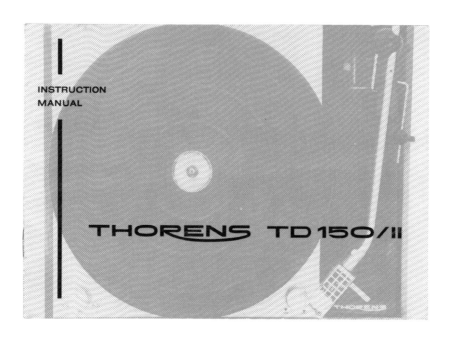

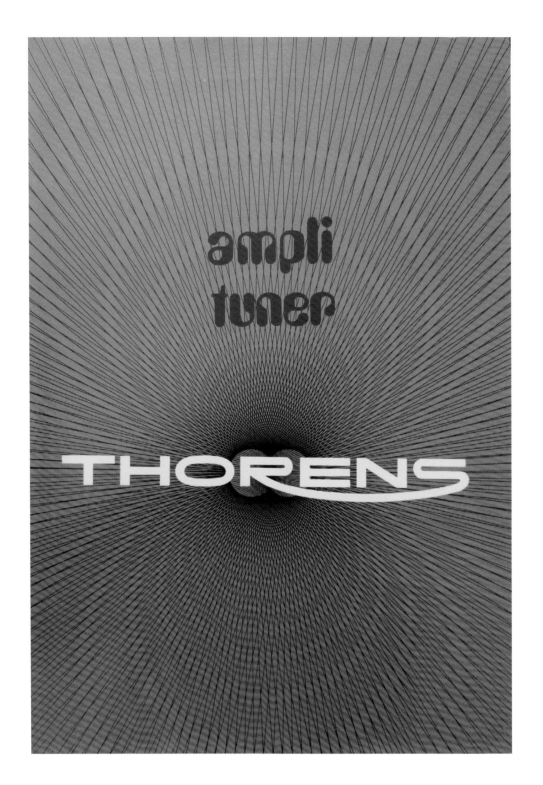

ampli
tuner

THORENS

TOSHIBA

Yet another Japanese technology conglomerate. This one, Toshiba, started in 1875 making telegraph equipment. They went on to be electronics innovators, making masses of useful kit, including the first Japanese microwave (1959), colour video phone (1971), word processor (1978) and personal laptop computer (1986). In the UK the company probably reached a commercial peak in the mid-1980s with the unforgettable 'Ello Tosh Got A Toshiba' campaign, written by Dave Trott and sung by Ian Dury. Toshiba still thrives today, currently employing nearly 120,000 people.

TRIPLETONE

This UK company started out as Servio Radio, but renamed itself in 1956 after its popular 'Tripletone' valve amplifier. Sadly they never really recovered from a fire at their Wimbledon premises in 1976.

1970-71

TRIO

It's the Kasuga Radio Company from Japan again with its confusing past (see Kenwood p110). The company named itself Trio in 1960, then in 1986, when brand recognition of Kenwood surpassed that of Trio, Trio called itself Kenwood. I'm still a bit confused.

ültra

the set you <u>can</u> judge by appearances

ULTRA

Wireless expert Teddy Rosen started what was later to become Ultra back in 1920 (he had originally used the name Ultra for one of his loudspeaker models). This British company manufactured products for domestic, commercial and military clients, producing a wide range of products from bomb doors for aircraft to portable radios and, in the early 1950s, television sets. In 1961, the domestic element of Ultra was sold to Thorn EMI who continued to use the Ultra name. The remaining part of the company went on to form Ultra Electronics Ltd, eventually becoming a large and important electronic defence and security firm. I thought it was a bit odd when I began researching them and warships and tanks started popping up.

M HARVEY

ultra

the set you can judge by appearances

UTAH

This company were the brand of choice throughout the 1960s and 1970s for the enthusiastic hi-fi DIY'er who wanted to build their own speaker cabinets.

VELODYNE

Launched in 1983 in Silicon Valley, their specialist low-frequency sound and subwoofer technology was specifically aimed at the music and home theatre market. Today their original idea has been exploited by many companies, but Velodyne were there first with the dynamic subwoofer setup.

VERIT

A Sun Valley speaker firm originally founded in 1967 as Tangiers Industries. After some considerable research, I think you'd need to employ a good detective like Kojak to find out what actually happened to this company.

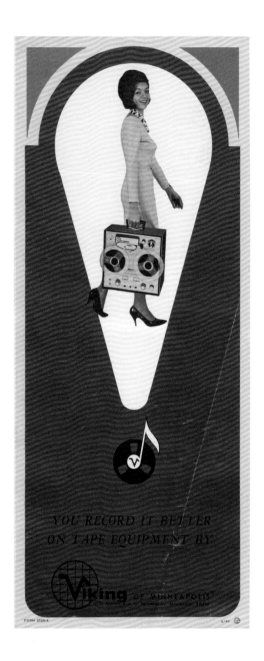

YOU RECORD IT BETTER
ON TAPE EQUIPMENT BY.

880 STEREO

FINEST PORTABLE TAPE RECORDER

IN ITS CLASS

Incorporates all the features of 88 Stereo Compact plus a 10 watt solid state stereo power amplifier with stereo headphone jack and monitor volume control and detachable sattelite speakers.

Carry everywhere for "on location" recording or connect to home music system.

880 Stereo, complete $439.95

Hysteresis synchronous capstan motor optional at extra cost.

230 volt operation optional at extra cost.

807 TURNTABLE
OF THE
TAPE AGE

Enjoy the superior quality of tapes with the convenience of phonograph records.

Connect a Viking 807 to your music system and play stereo or monaural tapes, full, half or quarter track at 3¾ or 7½ ips. Automatic shut-off, cueing, fast forward and rewind features included for highest operating convenience.

807 complete with walnut base $124.95

VIKING

Peter Rasmussen started the American company Viking as a tool and machine manufacturer in 1946. By 1947 they'd made a really cool popcorn machine called the Minit. Their first reel to reel hits the world in 1957 and by the mid-1960s they had begun to produce tape players for the professional field. The company was sold to Telex in 1966.

VICTOR

This is the brand name of JVC in Japan (see p102), with items being sold using both the Victor name and with the HMV dog 'Nipper' as can be seen on this brochure. Just check out the boombox on a skateboard...

Victor

音楽をおもいっきり呼吸しよう。われらミュージックフリーク。
メタルテープ対応機からコンパクトタイプまで、いい音あるあるビクター。

stereo . . .
distinctively
yours

Weathers

Harmony
Stereo
Speakers

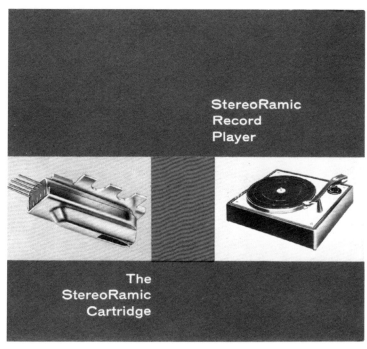

StereoRamic
Record
Player

The
StereoRamic
Cartridge

WEATHERS

In 1929, American electrical engineer Paul Weathers started working for RCA (see p160) on sound for talking movies, going on to help create the public address system for the 1939 New York World's Fair. After striking out on his own in 1950, Weathers created a series of fine and progressively engineered cartridges, tonearms and turntables, many of which are still highly sought-after today.

WESTREX

A subsidiary of Western Electric, the original manufacturers of cinema horn speakers in the 1920s, with technology that to some, still remains unmatched. Westrex were heavily involved with the cinema industry, developing sound-recording equipment for film, amplification systems for theatres etc. The company was sold to Litton Industries in the late 1950s.

FROM WORLD-FAMOUS WESTREX   'PACK-UP-AND-GO' PUBLIC ADDRESS EQUIPMENT

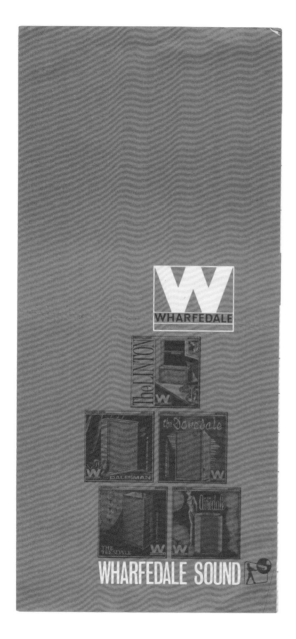

WHARFEDALE'S
Guide to choosing speakers.

WHARFEDALE

This company is named after the Wharfedale Valley in Yorkshire, home of Gilbert Briggs, an ex-textile factory worker with a love of classical music, who established Wharfedale Wireless Works in 1932. A keen hobbyist, he built his first speaker in his basement, becoming an expert in the field and writing a number of books on the subject. In the 1950s he teamed up with amplifier manufacturer Peter Walker (see QUAD, p156) on a series of concerts inviting audiences to compare live and recorded music, while simultaneously promoting their products. According to legend, his demonstration concert at the newly built Royal Festival Hall in 1954 was a complete sell-out (they also played Carnegie Hall in New York City). Wharfedale still has a fine reputation for speaker technology and is currently owned by the International Audio Group in China.

How to get
the best from your
Linton 2 Speakers

WHARFEDALE

XP SERIES SPEAKERS

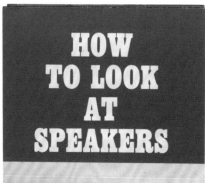

HOW TO LOOK AT SPEAKERS

BY
wigo
PRONOUNCE IT WEEGO

You won't buy a WIGO for looks

There are no gimmicks with WIGO

. . . because Wigo doesn't try to impress you with cosmetic frills that may look good, but only increase costs without adding to either value or performance.

Take a tip from WIGO

. . . like the experienced audiophile, judge a speaker by the way it sounds to your ears. You'll find the best sounding speakers are those benefiting from superior engineering skillfully applied to the finest available materials.

. . . instead, you'll find such essentials as rugged cast aluminum frames integrated with heavy magnet assemblies for extra rigidity, constant response voice coils, climate-proof cone suspensions and hyperbolic cone designs . . . all found elsewhere only in far costlier speakers.

It all adds up with WIGO

WINDSOR
Laboratory Series

High Fidelity
Loudspeaker Systems

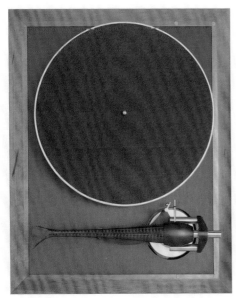

Craftsmanship
Innovation
Leading edge technology

WIGO

This German audio speaker company established in the 1960s is currently part of the Kenwood stable.

WINDSOR

There isn't a great deal of information on these Winsdor Laboratory Series speakers, although we've found out they were a pretty large size and they may well be a subsidiary of an American electronics firm called Shuco.

WILSON BENESCH

Founded in Sheffield in 1989, Wilson Benesch make very high-end audio products. They operate from a building formerly occupied by Batchelors, the company that gave us soup, then Cup-a-Soup.

Wollensak 3M COMPANY

From the bold new world of Wollensak sound

AUDIO CENTER SERIES

Stereo Tape Recorders

The Wollensak Audio Center Series is ideal for the audiophile or amateur interested in making truly professional recordings. The recorders feature three non-magnetizing heads and a two-motor drive to reduce wow and flutter. Its professional-type patch board helps you create special effects, such as reverberation, sound-on-sound, sound-with-sound, input mixing and more, with ease.

Wollensak 6350 audio center.
Four track stereo with snap-on acoustic suspension speakers. Built-in 62 Watt (IHF) component amplifier.

Wollensak 6150 tape track.
Four track stereo features fixed and controlled pre-amp outputs. Contained in a hand-rubbed walnut base.

Wollensak 6360 audio center.
Four track stereo with walnut oil-finished wood base. Separate acoustic suspension cube speakers (also available without speakers). Speakers may be ordered separately). Built-in 62 Watt (IHF) component amplifier.

Wollensak 6250 audio center.
Four track stereo with self-contained acoustic suspension speakers. Built-in 62 Watt (IHF) component amplifier.

for Professional Recordings

Wollensak audio center features: 4-Track stereophonic recording/playback • 4-Track monophonic recording/playback • 3 Speeds • 3 Heads • 2 Motors • Push-Button Tape Controls • Acoustic suspension speakers (6250/6350/6360) • All solid-state electronics • 62 Watts IHF stereo output with inputs for magnetic phono, tuner, microphone, auxiliary (6250/6350/6360). • Tape/source monitoring • Open-front trigrading • Record bias selector • Sound-on-sound, sound-with-sound, reverberation, enhanced mono recording • Separate bass and treble controls • Separate record level controls • 4-digit tape counter • Electro-dynamic braking • Automatic shut-off • Pause control • Stereo headphone output • Non-magnetizing heads • Low impedance wide range microphones (6250/6350/6360) • Vertical or horizontal operation

WOLLENSAK

This American audio visual company began making components for stills cameras in 1902. In partnership with the Revere Camera Company, they produced a range successful 8mm film cameras in the 1950s and early 1960s. As part of 3M (see Scotch p178) their robust reel to reel tape recorders were practically bullet proof and therefore the defacto choice of schools and offices. The company closed in 1972.

New Wollensak
Cartridge Tape Recorder plays anywhere on its own batteries.

What you want is a Wollensak!

YAMAHA TC800GL

High-performance stereo cassette deck with less than 0.06% wow & flutter, radical new easy-operation design, Dolby system, pitch control and automatic recording start.

YAMAHA

The Yamaha Corporation is the world's largest musical instrument manufacturer, established in 1887 to produce reed organs. By 1900 piano manufacturing had begun and the first cranking phonograph by 1922, while motorcycles were speeding out of the factory by 1954. They have a number of impressive innovations under their belt, including the origins of the first compact disc recorder and the first commercially successful synthesiser (the DX-7). The company currently employs close to 30,000 people.

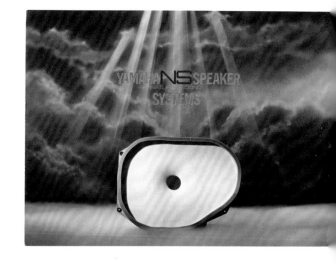

Performance/Convenience
Home Stereo Centers

MSC-3
MSC-5AR
MSC-5B
MC-40

YAMAHA NS SYSTEMS
NATURAL SOUND

model A279W
THE ADVENTURER

Polystyrene with Grained Walnut Color
Covering, Model A279W

ZENITH
BATTERY-OPERATED
SOLID-STATE AM
CLOCK RADIO

Compact design cabinet with swivel base, comes complete with batteries for clock and radio

• Turns 360° on a Swivel Base • Wakes You with Music • Precision Vernier Tuning
• Leak-Resistant Battery Compartment • Luminous hands

The quality goes in before the name goes on®

ZENITH

Here I was thinking Zenith were a Swiss watch company that made some pretty cool, innovative wrist watches. Then I found out that the reason they couldn't really sell their watches in America was because they had a long-running ding-dong legal battle with Zenith Electronics from Illinois. They made the slightly ridiculous thing you see here, a weird battery-operated clock speaker. But, they were also truly innovative, creating the first portable radio back in 1924, followed by push-button tuning in 1927. The company was bought by the South Korean conglomerate LG in 1999.

ATLANTA HIGH FIDELITY
MUSIC SHOW OF 1972

MERCHANDISE MART & PEACHTREE CENTER

FEBRUARY 18, 19, 20 & 21

Produced by M. Robert Rogers and Teresa Rogers

OFFICIAL PROGRAM PUBLISHED BY FORECAST FM, WASHINGTON, D.C.

THE RECORD OMNIBOOK · TURNTABLES · TONE ARMS AND CARTRIDGES · RECORD CLEANING EQUIPMENT ·

ENDORSED BY ELPA

Other books by Jonny Trunk / FUEL

First published in 2024

FUEL Design & Publishing
33 Fournier Street
London E1 6QE

fuel-design.com

Scans, research and text by Jonny Trunk
Retouching by Lili Martinez at Poporo Creative

Edited by Jonny Trunk, Damon Murray
and Stephen Sorrell
Designed by Murray & Sorrell FUEL

Printed in China
Distributed by Thames & Hudson / D. A. P.
ISBN: 978-1-7398878-1-0

Special thanks to the following amazing and generous
experts and dealers who helped:
Berris Conolly for his Gale brochure scan
Paddy and Keir at Whitaker Malem for their deep insider
knowledge and enthusiasm
J.A. Michell for lending me their rare brochures
Audio Gold for providing numerous brochures and the killer
Star Wars fact
Peter Kapos at Das Programm for the invaluable help and
access to their Braun archive